# PUERTO VALLARTA

2nd edition

Richard Bizier
Roch Nadeau

D0707011

ULYSSES
TRAVEL PUBLICATIONS
Travel better... enjoy more

| | | |
|---|---|---|
| **Author** | **Project Supervisor** | **Series Director** |
| Richard Bizier, | Daniel Desjardins | Claude Morneau |
| Roch Nadeau | *Asistants* | |
| *Collaboration* | Marc Rigole | **Production Director** |
| Paquerette Villeneuve | Christian Roy | Pascale Couture |
| Paul Haince | | |
| | **Cartography** | **Photography** |
| **Editing and Translation** | André Duchesne | *Cover Photo* |
| Danielle Gauthier | *Assistants* | Roch Nadeau |
| Tara Salman | Patrick Thivierge | |
| Sadia Mir | Line Magier | **Illustrations** |
| | | Lorette Pierson |
| **Layout** | **Artistic Director** | Sophie Matteau |
| Tara Salman | Patrick Farei - Atoll Dir. | |

**Thanks to** Guillermo Ponce, Director of the Office of Tourism of Mexico in Montréal; Letica Matus; Yolanda Franco, Director of the Secretariat of Tourism of the State of Jalisco in Puerto Vallarta; tour coordinators J. Ludwig Estrada Virgen and Alvaro Campos; Jorge Arturo Barrón Villalobos, Director of Communications and Public Relations and Carlos Torres Ramírez, Director of Marketing and Publicity, both at the Secretariat of Tourism of the State of Jalisco in Guadalajara; María De Lourdes Quintero Sànchez, tour coordinator; friends in Puerto Vallarta: Rita A. Kruz, Roger Dreier, Thierry Blouet and Jesús Botelle Sánchez.

## DISTRIBUTORS

**AUSTRALIA**: Little Hills Press, 11/37-43 Alexander St., Crows Nest NSW 2065, ☎ (612) 437-6995, Fax: (612) 438-5762

**BELGIUM AND LUXEMBOURG**: Vander, Vrijwilligerlaan 321, B-1150 Brussel, ☎ (02) 762 98 04, Fax: (02) 762 06 62

**CANADA**: Ulysses Books & Maps, 4176 Saint-Denis, Montréal, Québec, H2W 2M5, ☎ (514) 843-9882, ext.2232, 800-748-9171, Fax: 514-843-9448, www.ulysses.ca

**GERMANY AND AUSTRIA**: Brettschneider, Fernreisebedarf, Feldfirchner Strasse 2, D-85551 Heimstetten, München, ☎ 89-99 02 03 30, Fax: 89-99 02 03 31, Brettschneider_Fernreisebedarf@t-online.de

**GREAT BRITAIN AND IRELAND**: World Leisure Marketing, Unit 11, Newmarket Court, Newmarket Drive, Derby DE24 8NW, ☎ 1 332 57 37 37, Fax: 1 332 57 33 99, office@wlmsales.co.uk

**ITALY**: Centro Cartografico del Riccio, Via di Soffiano 164/A, 50143 Firenze, ☎ (055) 71 33 33, Fax: (055) 71 63 50

**NETHERLANDS**: Nilsson & Lamm, Pampuslaan 212-214, 1380 AD Weesp (NL), ☎ 0294-494949, Fax: 0294-494455, E-mail: info@nilsson-lamm.nl

**SCANDINAVIA**: Scanvik, Esplanaden 8B, 1263 Copenhagen K, DK, ☎ (45) 33.12.77.66, Fax: (45) 33.91.28.82

**SPAIN**: Altaïr, Balmes 69, E-08007 Barcelona, ☎ 454 29 66, Fax: 451 25 59, altair@globalcom.es

**SWITZERLAND**: OLF, P.O. Box 1061, CH-1701 Fribourg, ☎ (026) 467.51.11, Fax: (026) 467.54.66

**U.S.A.**: The Globe Pequot Press, 6 Business Park Road, P.O. Box 833, Old Saybrook, CT 06475, ☎ 1-800-243-0495, Fax: 800-820-2329, sales@globe-pequot.com

No part of this publication may be reproduced in any form or by any means, including photocopying, without the written permission of the publisher.
© July 1999, Ulysses Travel Publications.
All rights reserved    Printed in Canada    ISBN 2-89464-150-8

*"The Huichol is an ecologist by nature. The gods he worships, goddesses of water and corn, gods of air or rain, personify natural phenomena... When a Huichol dances, he taps his feet lightly, as if to caress the earth"*

– M. Delgado-Ramírez
Consulate General of Mexico in Montreal

# TABLE OF CONTENTS

## CATALOGUING

Bizier, Richard

      Puerto Vallarta

      2nd Edition
      (Ulysses Due South)
      Translation of: Puerto Vallarta
      Includes index

      ISBN 2-89464-150-8

1. Puerto Vallarta (Mexico) – Guidebooks. I. Nadeau, Roch. II. Title.
III. Series.

F1391.593B5913 1999    917.2'3504836    C99-940860-7

We acknowledge the financial support of the Government of
Canada through the Book Publishing Industry Development Program
(BPIDP) for our publishing activities.

# Canada

We would also like to thank SODEC for their financial support.

# LIST OF MAPS

# WRITE TO US

The information contained in this guide was correct at press time. However, mistakes can slip in, omissions are always possible, places can disappear, etc. The authors and publisher hereby disclaim any liability for loss or damage resulting from omissions or errors.

We value your comments, corrections and suggestions, as they allow us to keep each guide up to date. The best contributions will be rewarded with a free book from Ulysses Travel Publications. All you have to do is write us at the following address and indicate which title you would be interested in receiving (see the list at the end of guide).

**Ulysses Travel Publications**
**4176 Rue Saint-Denis**
**Montréal, Québec**
**Canada H2W 2M5**
**www.ulysses.ca**
**E-mail: guiduly@ulysses.ca**

# SYMBOLS

| | |
|---|---|
| 🚢 | Ulysses' favourite |
| ☎ | Telephone number |
| ⊨ | Fax number |
| ≡ | Air conditioning |
| ⊗ | Ceiling fan |
| ≈ | Pool |
| ♯ | Screen |
| ℜ | Restaurant |
| ⊚ | Whirlpool |
| ℝ | Refrigerator |
| K | Kitchenette |
| △ | Sauna |
| ⊘ | Exercise room |
| tv | Colour television |
| P | Parking |
| pb | Private bathroom |
| sb | Shared bathroom |
| ps | Private shower |
| bkfst | Breakfast |

## ATTRACTION CLASSIFICATION

| | |
|---|---|
| ★ | Interesting |
| ★★ | Worth a visit |
| ★★★ | Not to be missed |

## HOTEL CLASSIFICATION

Prices in the guide are for one room, double occupancy in high season.

| | |
|---|---|
| $ | $30 US or less |
| $$ | $30 to $50 US |
| $$$ | $50 to $70 US |
| $$$$ | $70 to $100 US |
| $$$$$ | $100 US or more |

## RESTAURANT CLASSIFICATION

| | |
|---|---|
| $ | $5 US or less |
| $$ | $5 to $10 US |
| $$$ | $10 to $20 US |
| $$$$ | $20 to $30 US |
| $$$$$ | $30 US or more |

Prices in the guide are for a meal for one person, excluding drinks and tip.

**All prices in this guide are in American dollars.**

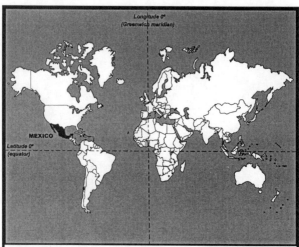

Longitude 0°
(Greenwich meridian)

MEXICO

Latitude 0°
(equator)

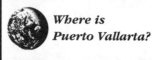

## Where is
## *Puerto Vallarta?*

**Mexico**

Capital: Mexico City
Population: 85,700,000 inhab.
Currency: Mexican peso
Area: 1,970,000 km²

**Puerto Vallarta**

Population: 123,560 inhab.

## PORTRAIT

**F**ounded in 1851 by the Sánchez family, Puerto Vallarta (pronounced PWEHR-to ba-YAR-ta) was still a simple hamlet a little over a century later, but has since become a world renowned beach resort. Even in the early days of Mexico's colonization, the *conquistadores* who explored this vast area of the Pacific littoral between the sea and the Sierra Madre mountain range were amazed at the beauty of its coastal scenery. If Puerto Vallarta seems like a jewel, as many proclaim, there is no doubt that it could find no lovelier setting than the state of Jalisco (pronounced kha-LEES-co). This part of Mexico has a rich historical past. The continuing archaeological digs being conducted here give us a glimpse into centuries-old Spanish culture and millennium-old native culture.

Different tourists judge Puerto Vallarta in different ways. First there are those who knew the town in its pre-Hollywood era, before it became famous as the setting for the film *The Night of the Iguana*, based on the play by Tennessee Williams, and starring Richard Burton and Ava Gardner in 1963. Then, of course, there are those who come without even considering the peaceful coastal village of not so long ago. Even if that earlier Puerto Vallarta probably exuded the charm of a veritable Garden of Eden, repeated bursts of hotel-building since that time have not tarnished its beauty.

Even after some renovation, this resort town has managed to preserve its old areas in the heart of the urban core. Apart from the inevitable architectural errors along the beach, modern hotel development has mostly taken place away from the centre of town — north of the airport; around the Marina Vallarta; along Highway 200 on the way south to Boca de Tomatlán, or on the northern periphery in a newly developed area called Nuevo Vallarta which extends across the boundary with the neighbouring state of Nayarit.

It's not at all surprising that more and more tourists and ordinary travellers have adopted Puerto Vallarta as a vacation destination. Mexicans themselves, given the chance to flee their urban environment, flock in great numbers to this stunning spot on the Pacific Riviera. Besides the fact that this busy coastal town arouses an irresistible attraction, it's the whole Puerto Vallarta region that attracts visitors. Whoever comes to Puerto Vallarta always dreams of returning. During and after the filming of *The Night of the Iguana*, this town witnessed the idyllic love affair between Richard Burton and Elizabeth Taylor, a romance as tumultuous as it was passionate. Their stay in Puerto Vallarta, where they decided to make their love-nest, had all the journalists and gossip columnists of the international press rushing to get here, providing a great deal of publicity for the city, especially among Americans.

## GEOGRAPHY

The Mexican republic, whose official name is *Estados Unidos Mexicanos* (United States of Mexico), is a federal entity formed by 31 states plus the Federal District, containing Mexico City. The country occupies much of the southern part of the North American continent. It has a 3,363-km border with the United States of America to the north, and also borders on Guatemala and Belize to the southeast. Its 10,000 km of coastline are washed by the waters of the Pacific Ocean, the Gulf of Cortés, the Gulf of Mexico and the Caribbean Sea.

Mexico has an area of 1,972,547 km$^2$ (760,695 mi$^2$) and a population of 93.7 million according to the 1994 census. About 217,000 km$^2$ of Mexican territory are suitable for agriculture.

The city of Puerto Vallarta is located on the west coast of the state of Jalisco. Jalisco is shaped like a crescent with its points turned toward the Pacific Ocean. It is bordered by the states of Nayarit and Durango to the northwest, Zacatecas and Aguascalientes to the centre-north, San Luis Potosí and Guanajuato to the northeast, and the states of Michoacán and Colima closing the loop from the centre-east to the southwest.

Jalisco has an area of 80,836 km$^2$ (31,174 mi$^2$) and a population of more than 8 million. The state capital is Guadalajara (pronounced gwa-da-la-KHA-ra), with a population of about 6 million, making it the second biggest city in Mexico. There are an estimated 200,000 people living around the Bahía de Banderas with 123,560 in Puerto Vallarta. This resort town faces the Bahía de Banderas (Bay of Flags), a majestic bay stretching 42 km from east to west and 32 km from north to south, making it the biggest natural bay in Mexico and one of the biggest on the planet.

The Sierra Madre del Sur, an imposing mountain range, crosses the state of Jalisco. Puerto Vallarta is perched between the foothills of these mountains and the vast beaches bathed by the emerald waters of the Pacific Ocean. Enjoying an ideal geographic location and magnificent scenery, Puerto Vallarta takes advantage of these undeniable assets, which help it draw no fewer than two million visitors each year.

The state of Jalisco boasts Mexico's second biggest lake, the Laguna de Chapala (a tiny portion of which lies in the state of Michoacán); the lake has an area of 2,460 km$^2$ and sits at an altitude of 1,500 km.

## Geology

Mexico has a complex, almost tortured topography. The country has the full variety of geological formations to be found in the western part of the North American continent. According to one account, when King Ferdinand of Spain asked Hernán Cortés for a description of Mexico's topography, Cortés took a sheet of paper and, after crumpling it between his hands, handed it to the monarch with just one comment: "Here it is, Your Excellency".

This mountainous, uneven country is crossed by many rivers, but their weak currents and unreliable flows render them unnavigable. The highlands of the central plateau, accounting for 60% of Mexico's land mass, are flanked by the eastern and western Sierra Madre mountain ranges. Most of the big volcanoes are found in the southern part of the country.

## FAUNA AND FLORA

Flora and fauna in Mexico are highly diversified. This unique biodiversity has drawn the attention of scholars from around the world. Biologists have found 15% more types of vertebrates in Mexico than in the United States, 15% of the country's animal and plant species are found nowhere else on earth. There are more than 11,000 species of birds and about 1,500 species of land and sea mammals, plus many reptiles and amphibians. An impressive 30,000 different kinds of plants representing all species can be found in Mexico.

*Iguana*

**Parrots**

---

## Fauna

---

Mexico is the country where turkeys and guinea-pigs originated. It is also the realm of the graceful jaguar, the puma, the lynx, the ocelot, the tapir, the iguana, the turtle, and a multitude of snakes, including the famous boa constrictor. It is home to the eagle, the falcon, the colourful red macaw, the parrot and numerous other species.

Some species are threatened. Among the main causes of this are deforestation, hunting, industrial pollution, and population growth that has seen urban areas extend into very fragile ecological zones. Some zoos with settings that respect the environment and the natural habitat of the animals have been set up to protect certain endangered species.

## The Eagle, Mexico's National Emblem

An eagle perched on a cactus and devouring a snake has been Mexico's official heraldic emblem since 1821. According to legend, this national emblem, which is found on the flag, postage stamps, coins, public buildings and just about everywhere else in Mexico, has its origins in a prophecy. Revealed by an Aztec god, this prophecy promised prosperity and glory to the precise spot where someone would see an eagle devouring a serpent on a cactus growing out of a rock. This occurred on a little island in Lake Texcoco. It was on this spot that the Aztecs founded Tenochtitlán (from the Aztec words *tetl* for rock and *nochtli* for cactus), the fabulous imperial city that was discovered by the Spanish and that would become Mexico City.

## Flora

The tropical climate enables tens of thousands of plant species to thrive. Regardless of the region, Mexico has very distinctive flora. The country harbours many species of trees often exploited by the forest industry. These include red oak, Campeche logwood, mahogany, sandalwood, rosewood, pine, eucalyptus, ebony, avocado and cedar.

It is interesting to note that even the most arid land can quench the thirst of Mexicans. Several varieties of the agave family of cactuses grow in the desert and provide the base for most of Mexico's popular liquors.

Among the many plants originating in Mexico are cacao, nasturtium, sunflower, *chayote*, vanilla, *alkékenge*, Barbary fig, papaya, guava, avocado (*ahacatl* in Aztec) and poinsettia. Even before the arrival of the Spanish conquistadores, most of Mexico's native peoples were familiar with peanuts, corn, tomatoes, and hundreds of varieties of peppers, plus squashes and beans. Agriculture has always played an important role in the Mexican economy; fruits, vegetables, plants, seeds and exotic products are all exported north to the United States and Canada, especially during the winter.

## A Story About Chocolate

The Aztecs prepared a sacred drink that they called *tchocolatl* and regarded as an elixir of the gods. In 1519, at the very time the Spaniard Hernán Cortés discovered the fabulous city of Tenochtitlán (now Mexico City), Emperor Moctezuma offered him the famous *tchocolatl*, which was then less refined than what we know today. One account tells us that Cortés found this mixture, spiked with a bit of cinnamon, to be downright horrible! What induced Cortés to adopt cocoa in spite of this? Well, it seems that one of the virtues the Aztecs attributed to chocolate was an ability to approach women more easily. There is no need to ask any longer why the Spanish persisted so stubbornly with their "conquests"! Cortés did not hesitate to send cocoa to King Ferdinand and to Spain, where sugar was added to it. Later, the infatuation with cocoa spread quickly across Europe.

### Cocoa Production

The cacao tree, from which cocoa is extracted, originates in Mexico. The flowers and fruits of the cacao tree, unlike other fruit trees, grow around the trunk and not on the branches. Each of the oval-shaped fruits, or pods, contains seeds, often called beans. There can be 20 to 40 of these in each pod. Once the beans are extracted, a long process begins. First the beans are left to ferment, allowing them to develop their flavour. Next they are meticulously sorted, washed in a centrifuge, and then dried and roasted. The beans are then ground, forming a "mash" that is converted into a liquid mass. It is from this substance that cocoa is produced.

Submitted to very high pressures, the "mash" is pressed and what flows from this operation yields a dark brown cocoa paste; the other part, the "fat", becomes creamy white cocoa butter. This butter is used in the preparation of white chocolate. Lecithin, an artificial emulsifier, is commonly used to replace cocoa butter in most chocolate products.

# HISTORY

Puerto Vallarta faces the magnificent Bahía de Banderas (Bay of Flags) on Mexico's Pacific coast. This bay is bordered on the north by the Vallejo mountain range, at the foot of which lies the fishing village of Punta Mita. The bay extends south to Cabo Corrientes, where the last foothills of the Sierra Cuale stand.

The first Europeans to land there were Spanish soldiers in the 16th century on their way back from expeditions to Baja California (or the Isle of Pearls, as they then called it). They stopped here to get fresh supplies of water, firewood and food, and these hospitable and fertile shores were mentioned more than once in documents from that period.

In those times of piracy, it was necessary for ships returning from the Philippines to find safe havens. They also needed to stop for repairs and to seek fresh supplies, and maybe even (history doesn't say) for sailors to relax again after their interminable crossing of the Pacific Ocean. It was the Spanish captain Pedro de Unamuno who, after returning from an expedition to the Philippines in 1587, first suggested establishing a colony in the bay. Other famous navigators like Sebastián Vizcaino, López de Vicuna and Gonzalo de Francía, after checking the bay's many advantages themselves, suggested setting up a colonization post there, although they had no greater success in bringing this about.

It is known there was a shipyard in the bay in 1664 (probably at the current site of Mismaloya), where two boats were built for Bernardo Bernal de Pinadero, who wanted to colonize the Isle of Pearls (Baja California). During the next two centuries, official documents and logbooks made frequent references to the whaling ships and other fishing vessels that landed in the Bahía de Banderas. At the time, the bay was often called Bahía de los Jorobados because of the many long-finned whales that could be seen there.

In the 19th century, the loading and unloading of provisions and materials destined for the companies exploiting the Guale and San Sebastian mines was carried out at Puerto Vallarta, or rather Las Peñas, as it was then called. In the middle of the century, Don Guadalupe Sánchez Torres, born in Cihuatlán in the state of Jalisco, began regular salt deliveries to the back-country mines, which required large quantities of salt to refine their silver. Don Guadalupe and his men built temporary shelters out of tree trunks and palm leaves to rest in while the salt was being unloaded and shifted to mule for transport to the mines.

In 1851, Don Guadalupe settled for good with his family at Las Peñas, which he called Las Peñas de Santa María de Guadalupe in honour of Our Lady of Guadalupe, whose feast day fell on December 12, the date of their arrival. Other families followed his example, gradually transforming the village's economy. The salt trade continued, slowly augmented by agriculture and stock breeding. We also know that German, French and English ships occasionally stopped to look for Brazil wood, a source of dye that was highly valued in Europe. In a report to the naval survey office, the English admiral George Dewey pointed to the existence of a little town called Las Peñas at the mouth of the Río Real where boats stopped to pick up dyewood. In 1874, the admiral returned aboard the *Narragansett* to observe the position of the stars, from Punta Mita to Tabo and at a point near Los Muertos beach, so that he could begin demarcating sites and drawing a map of the coast. By 1880, Las Peñas already had 1,500 inhabitants.

Five years later, on July 14, 1885, the port officially took the name Las Peñas as it became open to domestic coastal traffic. Nine days later, the first customs post was inaugurated there and, on October 31, the Mexican congressional bill 210 gave it an official political and judicial status.

In the late 19th and early 20th centuries, Las Peñas grew steadily, stimulated by collective effort and by the enthusiasm that Don Guadalupe continued to show. All the same, the town experienced its share of catastrophes in its development. In March 1883, a tidal wave ravaged the Bahía de Banderas. On May 6, 1800, a pot of boiling grease was overturned in a restaurant with a palm roof, causing a fire that destroyed more than half the houses. In 1911, a flood left more than 1,000 people in the street and, in 1922, a yellow fever epidemic killed 150 inhabitants. Nonetheless, during that period, the village gradually transformed itself into a viable economic centre. The first post office opened in March 1914, and six months later the telegraph was introduced. In May 1918, Jalisco state decree number 1889 raised the village's status to that of municipality. To honour the memory of Don Ignacio L. Vallarta, a famous lawyer and Jalisco governor, its name was changed to Puerto Vallarta, the same name it bears today.

In 1925, following the Montgomery Fruit Company's purchase of 28,000 hectares (69,000 acres) of land at Ixtapa, Puerto Vallarta enjoyed its first economic boom thanks to the many jobs offered by the big banana plantations. The company also built a railway to transport its bananas from Ixtapa to El Salado estuary, so they could be shipped to the United States. That lasted until 1938, when a new land reform law forced the company to leave Mexico. After that, people relied on local resources, growing corn, all sorts of beans, tobacco and a variety of oil-rich coconut all intended for the domestic market.

Around 1930, visitors from other parts of the country and from abroad began to come, and to come back, drawn by the beauty of the site and its peaceful atmosphere. Word spread little by little, attracting greater numbers of visitors each year.

In 1951, celebrations marking the centennial of Puerto Vallarta's founding drew international attention. Mexican navy ships came from Acapulco to give a 21-gun salute. Puerto Vallarta received a relic of the "True Cross", and Mexican writer Margarita Mantecón de Garza published the first book devoted to the history of the town.

The event that made Puerto Vallarta famous was the filming of the John Huston production, *The Night of the Iguana*, adapted from the play by Tennessee Williams and starring such famous actors as Richard Burton, Ava Gardner and Deborah Kerr. Visitors came by the thousands to see the filming and, with a little luck, to catch a glimpse of one of these stars. The publicity surrounding the film and the road improvements that followed kicked off the tourist boom in Puerto Vallarta. Three-star hotels were soon built, and the tourism industry began to replace agriculture as the main source of income.

From the time the first airplane landed in 1931, Puerto Vallarta has not stopped changing. There are now all categories of hotels, from affordable family inns to the most luxurious prestige establishments. Many airline companies link Puerto

Vallarta to other cities in Mexico, the United States, Canada and Europe. The port welcomes cruise ships almost every day. The new marina handles pleasure craft, and an excellent road network leads to Tepic, Guadalajara and the rest of Mexico. The population has grown at an impressive rate, rising from 12,500 in 1964 to more than 85,000 by 1994.

A substantial foreign community, made up mostly of Americans, Canadians and Europeans, lives in Puerto vallarta year-round and helps enliven local life. Puerto Vallarta's climate, as visitors are quick to notice, is pleasant at all times. The daytime maximum temperature is around 28° Celsius (83° Fahrenheit), and the sun shines every day except during the rainy season, which runs from mid-June to mid-September.

The city is surrounded by wonderful spots for picnicking or even for extending your stay in comfortable hotels where you can forget the rest of the world. The most popular excursions are along to coast to Bucerías, Mismaloya, Quimixto and Yelapa.

The Mexican government, along with the Jalisco and Nayarit states governments and private business, has put together a large-scale tourism development plan for the whole Bahía de Banderas region.

An international deep-sea fishing tournament is held each year at Puerto Vallarta during the first week of November. This well-known event draws passionate participants from all over Mexico, the United States and elsewhere. Puerto Vallarta is also a popular spot for conventions, seminars and conferences for all kinds of organizations. Among the most important of these gatherings was the August 1970 meeting between Mexican President Gustavo Díaz Ordaz and American President Richard Nixon. During that same year, a new shipping terminal and a new airport were inaugurated; both have been continuously improved and enlarged since then to meet a constantly growing demand.

In this same vein, Puerto Vallarta offers investors, businesspeople and tourists a very broad range of opportunities. As a holiday destination, it has become a favourite the world-over.

---

# POLITICS

---

Mexico is a presidential republic made up of 31 states and the Federal District, which contains Mexico City. The 1917 Constitution, which was drafted by Venustiano Carranza and Álvaro Obregón, is a socialist in nature. The President of the Republic and members of the Senate are elected to six-year terms, while members of the Chamber of Deputies are elected for three years.

The Federal Electoral Institute (IFE) is an independent organization with the mandate to oversee Mexico's elections. Five recognized political parties participate in national elections: the National Action Party (PAN), the Party of the Democratic Revolution (PRD), the Institutional Revolutionary Party (PRI), the Workers Party (PT) and the Mexican Green Ecologist Party (PVEM).

---

# THE ECONOMY

---

According to the latest statistics, Mexico's economy has been experiencing remarkable growth and President Ernest Zedillo's economic-reform program and austere fiscal and monetary policies alike have enabled the country to overcome the crisis of the mid-1990s and to lay down solid foundations for long-term economic growth. After declining 6.2% in 1995, the real GDP grew 5.1% in 1996 and 7.3% in 1997. Mexican exports amounted to $8.4 billion US in December 1996, representing an increase of 24.6 per cent over December 1995. Imports, too, are constantly rising, totalling $8.1 billion in December 1996, or 28.8% compared to 1995. This economic recovery has resulted in the lowest unemployment rate in the last few years at only 4.1%. The drop in inflation is another one of the beneficial effects of this economic upswing. In January 1996, the National Consumer Price Index (NCPI) increased by 2.57 per cent over December 1995.

Petroleum remains one of Mexico's greatest natural resources, despite a fall in oil revenues. The country's subsoil also contains substantial deposits of iron, silver, copper, gold, coal, lead, uranium and zinc; some of these deposits are mined by state-owned companies. Since Mexico became part of the North American Free Trade Agreement, the country has seen a growth in its exports to the United States and Canada, especially manufactured goods and food products. Beef and corn production are mostly destined for the domestic market. The tourism industry is another important contributor to the Mexican economy.

While tourism contributes 54 per cent to the total economy of the Costa Norte region, thanks to the famous seaside resort of Puerto Vallarta, this part of the State of Jalisco is essentially agricultural — as can be attested by the following quantities (in tons per hectare) of crops produced:

Corn: 3,298
Beans: 1,903
Watermelons: 617
Mangos: 200
Bananas (plantains): 65
Papayas: 51
Coconuts: 17
*Nanches* (small yellow fruit): 10

Supplementing the agricultural economy is cattle, veal, pork, poultry and dairy-cow breeding, which yield revenues of a few tens of thousands of pesos for their producers.

## NATIONAL INFRASTRUCTURE

Mexico boasts 243,785 kilometres of roads (highways and major roads) and 26,613 kilometres of railways, 50 international airports, 33 national airports and, along the coasts, 140 bustling seaports. Lastly, close to 9 million telephone lines are in use in the country.

## THE PEOPLE

About 60% of the Mexican population is made up of *mestizos*, people of mixed Amerindian and European descent. About 30% are native people and the remaining 10% mostly of European origin. In addition to pronounced demographic growth, Mexico is seeing a major exodus of its rural populations to the cities.

## Language

Spanish is the official language of Mexico. In certain regions, native languages are commonly spoken by large portions of the local population.

Mexicans appreciate efforts by visitors to speak Spanish. This attitude helps create a friendlier climate that can lead to long-lasting friendships.

## Education

Although education must be secular, the Mexican Constitution guarantees freedom of religion. Basic education consists of nine years of compulsory schooling (primary and secondary). State education is free, and 27.8 million students, or 92% of the population under the age of 15 attend school. The Mexican government has made enormous efforts toward education. Six per cent of the GDP is allocated toward education and school textbooks are freely distributed annually for primary schools.

## Health

In 1995, the country had 113.4 physicians, 187.2 nurses and 85.3 hospital beds for every 100 000 inhabitants.

## Religion

The Catholic religion in Mexico shows strong Aztec origins. In the early days of the Spanish conquest, the invaders (*conquistadores*) levelled Amerindian temples and built Christian churches atop the ruins to impose their "new" religious beliefs. As a small consolation, natives were able to retain certain religious chants, as long as their prayers were directed to Christ and to the "true" saints of the Roman Catholic church. On the

other hand, many natives saw Jesus as a reincarnation of Quetzalcoatl, their Supreme Being. For many others, it was not Spanish colonization that gave the Catholic religion to the natives but rather the Virgin of Guadalupe, who appeared before Juan Diego, from the village of Tepeyac, about 5 km north of Mexico City's *zócalo*.

The legend goes that early one morning on December 8, 1531, an Aztec peasant named Juan Diego was on his way to the church of Santiago de Tlatelolco to attend Mass. On his way, as he passed near the Tepeyac hill, he heard sweet music and then a voice asking him in Nahuatl, his native tongue, "My son, Juan, where are you headed?" Surprised, he turned around and suddenly saw the hill enveloped in dazzling light. "I'm going to Mass", he replied as he stepped toward the spot from which this very comforting voice emanated. It was there, at the top of this mound, that Juan saw a lady who told him she was Mary, the Immaculate Virgin. (This occurred more than three centuries before the Virgin of Lourdes appeared before little Bernadette Soubirous in France.) It was the first of a series of apparitions by the Virgin to Juan Diego, and the first on this continent that Europeans called the New World.

During the first apparition, Mary confided to Juan Diego that she saw herself as the Protector of the native people, and she asked that a chapel be built for her at this very spot. In the following days, Juan requested of the bishop of Mexico, Juan de Zummarraga, that the wish of the Virgin be granted. Sceptical at first, the prelate asked Juan to seek proof from the so-called Virgin confirming her authenticity, which the peasant did during the second apparition. After talking with Juan Diego, the Virgin told him to bring the gullible archbishop the multitude of roses she had made appear at the site. Filling his toga with these sweet-smelling and miraculous roses, our Aztec hero rushed back to Mexico City. There, before the dumbfounded bishop, he let fall a shower of roses such as had never been seen. Moreover, a portrait of the Virgin appeared on his toga, with the physiognomy and skin tone of a native. After seeing this, Juan de Zummarraga readily agreed to acquiesce to Juan's demand for a chapel dedicated to the Virgin, thus giving natives from around the country a spot where they could worship their highly venerated Protector.

Mexico's patron saint is thus an unmistakably Amerindian virgin, and Nuestra Señora de Guadalupe is an authentically Mexican mythical product. However, the Mexican political system is secular. It was only during Pope John Paul II's last official visit to Mexico that this 95% Catholic country decided to establish diplomatic relations with the Vatican. Until then, Mexico was the only Spanish-speaking country in the Americas whose government did not officially recognize the Vatican.

PORTRAIT

## CULTURE

The main civilizations to occupy what is now Mexican territory in the millennium preceding the birth of Jesus Christ were the Olmecs, the Mayans, the Toltecs and the Aztecs. It was the Aztecs who faced the task of "receiving" the Spanish. All these groups had devised calendars, all had social structures linked to their religious traditions, all knew how to build monuments, and all were skilled craftsmen. The Olmec priests (1,200 B.C. to 200 B.C.) were both artists and scholars; they knew the concept of zero and designed imposing buildings. The Mayans came from the south, making their influence felt until the decline of their civilization in the 15th century; they had complex mathematical and astrological systems, and the many cities they inhabited bear witness to their genius. The Aztecs, who came from the north, founded the city of Tenochtitlán in 1325 (now Mexico City), which would deeply impress the Spanish with its temples and pyramids.

Other lesser known groups also settled in various parts of the country, whose topographic complexity, with its volcano-strewn highlands, hard-to-reach mountains and tortuous rivers, enabled them to subsist apart from attempts at expansion by the powerful empires that preceded the arrival of the Spanish conquistadores.

Throughout this time, the country's disconnected geography imposed a form of autarky on the native peoples as a whole. This state of affairs strengthened their respective cultures and protected them from invasion and domination. These ancient cultures, some of which have never been subjugated, still survive in startling ways. As present-day mirrors of a distant past, they create many doubts among contemporary intellectuals and writers who wonder about their origins and their future.

The novelist Carlos Fuentes expresses Mexican intellectuals' uneasy feeling about the past especially well in his works such as *Tiempo Mexicano*. The poet Octavio Paz, winner of the Nobel Prize for Literature in 1980, addresses this same theme in *Piedra del Sol*.

Among the peoples whose presence still forms part of Mexico's current ethnic spectrum, the Huicholes are one group that stands out. Even if there are only about 10,000 of them left, they have managed to maintain a solid heritage.

## Huichol Culture

The Bahía de Banderas, or Bay of Flags, named after the banners unfurled by the Spanish warriors, is shaped on the map like a parrot. In the most sheltered part of the this bay is the city of Puerto Vallarta. The natives living there are mostly Huicholes, as well as a few Coras. At the northern edge of the "beak" is Puerto Mita, whose name comes from *mitlán*, a word coined at a time when nobody imagined there could be other lands across the ocean and whose meaning in the Huichol language is "the end of the world and the edge of the unknown". Huicholes still come there today to celebrate weddings.

The Huicholes are rather shy and live in small groups, both in Puerto Vallarta and in spots scattered across the state of Jalisco. They live in adobe houses with thatched roofs. These houses have only one door and few windows or none at all. The walls stay cool in the summer and provide protection from the cold in the winter. The Huicholes grow corn and sell handicrafts that bring in pesos, which have replaced cacao as a means of exchange.

Thanks to their isolation, their art has kept its original purity, and the government of Jalisco State has helped promote it. This art is characterized by the exuberance and audacity of its colours and by a stylization divided equally between abstract notions and forces inspired by nature, brought together without volume or perspective on a single surface.

Their special way of alternating strands of coloured wool on wax-coated wooden panels gives their famous wishing tables a unique character. As for their traditional garb, men's clothing is more elaborate than women's clothing, for it symbolizes the place held by the wearer in the religious hierarchy and confers the right, at its highest level, to wear eagle or parrot feathers. In the current style, men carry small, richly brocaded purses and palm-frond hats, while women wear scarves with pearl-adorned fringes that they call *quechquemitl*.

The Huicholes continue to observe the tradition of the annual pilgrimage to places where *peyotl* grows. This is a cactus that grows wild in the mountains of the hinterland, especially at Viricota, near Real de Catorce, in the area around San Luis de Potosí. They go to chew this cactus in the hope of communicating with their gods in ceremonies whose rituals are unchanged. According to the French poet Henri Michaux, who described the effects in *Connaissance par les Gouffres* (Knowledge Across the Chasms), this causes "the orchestra of an immense inner life" to gush forth. The pilgrimage there and back by the priest and by the worshippers who accompany him can take 40 days, passing through a desert area with only the most basic of transport facilities. Needless to say, the site is a holy place for the Huicholes, and each of them is required to participate in this pilgrimage at least once during a lifetime.

The fascinating colours of Huichol art have been attributed to the sharp vision that develops after consuming *peyotl*. Perfected by centuries of religious, cultural and social tradition, this art has become a living source of nation-wide inspiration, as shown for example in the emblem of the 1968 Olympic Games in Mexico City.

"The Huichol is an ecologist by nature", says Señor Delgado Ramírez, the Mexican consul-general in Montréal and a descendant of Huicholes himself. "When a Huichol dances, he taps his foot gently, as if to caress the earth".

The Arte Mágico Huichol gallery in Puerto Vallarta (see p 162) has a permanent exhibition of some of Huichol works. The

## Mariano Azuela

Born in Lagos de Mareno in 1873, Mariano Azuela remains the most famous writer to originate from Jalisco. After studying medicine at the University of Guadalajara, young Azuela chose to return to his home town to practise his profession.

In 1896, Azuela — who was then only 23 years old — published his first collection of literary essays. He soon made a name for himself and, deriving inspiration from the great historic events of his time, became, for many of his compatriots, "the greatest novelist of the Mexican Revolution". Like many young people of his generation, Azuela criticized the dictatorship of General Porfirio Díaz, who ruled Mexico notoriously from 1876 to 1911. That same year, Azuela was appointed Director of Education of the State of Jalisco. After his friend President Francisco I. Madero, who liberated the country from Díaz's hold, was assassinated in 1913 by supporters of counter-revolutionary Victoriano Huerta, Azuelo joined the forces of Pancho Villa as an army medical officer. This was indeed a tumultuous period for Mexico. Madero's assassination gave rise to civil war and American military intervention (1914-1917), while at the same time, Emilio Zapata was wreaking havoc with his agrarian revolution, in the southern part of the country. An idealist and humanist, Azuela was disappointed with the turn of events. He thus sought exile in El Paso, Texas, where he wrote *Los de abajo* (The Underdogs). This work was published in Mexico nine years later and was hailed the greatest novel of the Mexican Revolution.

After his return from exile, Azuela settled in Mexico City, where he resumed writing while providing medical care to the poor. He died in 1952.at the mouth of the Río Real

writer Iritemai Pacheco Salvador has gone about collecting Huichol tales, which he has begun to publish in bilingual format by translating the Huichol hieroglyphic language into Spanish.

## Other Cultural Contributions

Huichol culture is not the only one you'll notice in Puerto Vallarta. The Virgin of Guadalupe church, although it dates only from the early 20th century, offers a faithful portrayal of the architectural styles used since the arrival of the Spanish and the introduction of Catholicism. The church is dedicated to the patron saint of Mexico, the Virgin of Guadalupe, whose feast day is December 12. This dark-skinned virgin was seen in an apparition by Juan Diego on the hill where the Aztecs honoured Tonantizín, the mother of their gods. The virgin is symbolic of the osmosis between the old and new religions. The church is topped by a crown that some say evokes the crown of Empress Charlotte, wife of the unfortunate Emperor Maximilian.

Strolling along the *malecón*, the long seaside promenade, you will come across several contemporary sculptures, the most famous of which is a bronze object portraying a *caballito de mar* (seahorse) being ridden by a naked child and standing nearly three metres high. A naive fresco by Manuel Lepe presents the history of Puerto Vallarta since its founding and adorns the steps of the city hall.

Frescoes and paintings generally executed in a very fresh style are found in many restaurants in Puerto Vallarta. In effect, colour is a cultural element used abundantly in day-to-day decoration.

## Archaeology

Inhabited for nearly 20 centuries, the whole area around the Bahía de Banderas is rich in treasures of the Huichol, Cora and other cultures. Substantial archaeological digs are being carried out methodically in the state of Jalisco to preserve the many traces of the past in this area, which may have had as many as 100,000 inhabitants before the arrival of the Spanish. The items that have been discovered include funeral vases, ceramic heads, household objects, jewellery and weapons, with arrowheads among them. Puerto Vallarta's Museo del Cuale, located on an island in the middle of the eponymous river, exhibits a modest assortment that nonetheless is worth visiting.

This museum, along with bigger museums in Guadalajara and Tepic, is run by the National Institute of Anthropology and History.

## FOOD AND DRINK

Juan Sosa and Hildebia Ávalos run the **Café de Olla** on Calle Basilio Badillo (see p 139). Mexicans adore soups with a chicken broth base and garnishes of rice, vegetables, meat, corn and so on. This spot makes excellent soups, and its dishes are authentic. It serves several different kinds of tortillas, thin corn-based pancakes that are a staple in the daily diet. Tortillas can be eaten on their own, or become *tacos* when they are rolled around *guacamole* (seasoned mashed avocado), various meats, red or green tomato sauce, hot peppers or various other fillings. Stuffed tortillas, baked and sometimes covered with melted cheese, are called *enchiladas*. They are called *quesadillas* when served as a sandwich. Don't confuse *tacos* with *tostadas*, which are fried tortillas sometimes served as an appetizer with cocktails.

Meats, fish and seafood are grilled outdoors on the barbecue. Among the house delicacies are chicken or beef baked in a banana leaf with cornmeal (*tamal en hoja de plátano*) and peppers stuffed with cheese (*chile relleno*).

### Traditional Cooking

The outdoor terrace at La Palapa (see p 140) on Los Muertos beach, where you can eat with your feet in the warm sand. This ideal site is a dream spot for breakfast. *Huevos divorciados*, a copious morning dish consisting of two fried eggs on tortillas accompanied by a sauce of green and red tomatoes, refried beans and *guacamole*, is served here. Alberto Pérez González, the manager of La Palapa, sings and plays the guitar. Sitting so close to the ocean, customers enjoy fresh fish and seafood, prepared a multitude of ways.

PORTRAIT

1 Cayenne pepper
2. Mirasol colorado
3. Small cayenne
   pepper
4. Dwarf cayenne
   pepper
5. Pequin
6. Hontaka
7. Ancho
8. Güero
9. Mulato

---

## Creative Cooking

---

Mexico's artistic vitality dazzles the visitor; Mexican cuisine enchants the palate. Two chefs have contributed to Puerto Vallarta's gourmet reputation. One is Thierry Blouet, of the Café des Artistes (see p 136), on Calle Guadalupe Sánchez, and the other is Roger Dreier, of Chez Roger (see p 135), on Calle Agustín Rodríguez. They explore everything wonderful that Mexico has to offer, creating unusual flavours that take a fresh new approach to, but also respect Mexican gastronomy.

When Chef Blouet prepares a crab and avocado salad a mango and cumin *vinaigrette*, it all becomes as Mexican and as harmonious as his stuffed pumpkin flower pancakes with corn and cheese accompanied by a Puebla pepper sauce. His recipes show his skill and his contribution to modern Mexican cooking.

Chef Dreier likes to innovate. His specialities wild game with Chihuahua berries and sea bream with giant prawns topped with hollandaise sauce flavoured with rock lobster.

## A Gourmet Tour of Puerto Vallarta

The waters of the Bahía de Banderas, teeming with fish, provide Puerto Vallarta with fish and seafood of unparalleled freshness. This Pacific port with its 300,000 inhabitants attracts artists who embellish the city's restaurants, gardens and parks with frescoes, murals, fountains and sculptures. With elegant art galleries lying cheek by jowl with restaurants, the talents of the chefs rivals those of the great artists.

Doing the rounds of Puerto Vallarta restaurants will not only familiarize you with fine Mexican food but also you to enjoy *haute cuisine* at one spot and family fare at another. The market offers various goods that were long familiar to the Aztecs and other native peoples in tropical areas of the continent, from Mexico to Peru, where potatoes, among other items, originated.

The Spanish made the humble spud known around the world, and they did the same with sweet potatoes, avocados, beans, corn, squash, hot peppers, tomatoes, green peppers, peanuts, pineapples, cocoa, vanilla, and turkeys, whose habitat stretched all the way along the Atlantic coast to New England. Other producers provide poultry, lamb, beef, pork and goat meat. As for fish and seafood, they are as fresh as can be in Puerto Vallarta.

## Mexican Wine

When the Jesuits introduced grape vines to Mexico in the 16th century, they created the first vineyard in North America. Mexican territory included vast areas with more temperate climates, in the present-day American states of Texas, California, New Mexico, Arizona, Utah, Nevada and portions of Colorado and Wyoming, all territories that would be annexed by the United States in the 19th century.

Tropical climates are not well suited to vineyards and, apart from table grapes, the importance of grape production forms an almost negligible part of Mexican agriculture and of the country's economy. Nonetheless, some areas at higher elevations, and also parts of the Baja California peninsula, manage to produce wines that cannot be considered top quality but are still quite drinkable. At the Café des Artistes in Puerto Vallarta, chef Thierry Blouet enjoys helping wine-lovers discover some of the better Mexican vintages. Some of these wines can be very good indeed, such as the very rare Cabernet Sauvignon from the dry lands of Baja California, which you should not hesitate to try.

PORTRAIT

## Mexican Liquors

Everywhere in Mexico's bars, cafés, restaurants and grocery stores, you will find a variety of liquors produced in different parts of the country.

### Mezcal

This liquor is produced by distilling the juice obtained from crushing the stem or the head of the agave cactus. This substance, fermented before distillation, is called *maguey*. The agave, a plant with a high fat content and long, sword-shaped leaves, is also used to prepare tequila. One noteworthy feature of mezcal, with its lovely golden colour, is that the bottle contains a little white worm of the sort found at the base of the agave's long pointed leaves, which store water for the plant. Mezcal is produced in Oaxaca state.

Mezcal is served on its own or, as with tequila, in cocktails such as the famous *margarita*.

### Coffee Liqueur (Kahlúa)

Produced originally in Mexico, this liqueur is made from coffee grains and is known around the world. It is even produced in Europe.

### Pulque

*Pulque* has a low alcohol content, but it has the strong flavour of overripe fruit, almost like an old apple. It is very popular in the countryside and is sold for just a few pesos. *Pulque*'s overly strong flavour prevents most foreigners from really appreciating this drink, which is produced from the head of one of the many varieties of agave.

### Rum

As in nearly every sugar-cane-growing tropical country, all types and qualities of rums are found in Mexico. These rums are less known compared to those produced in the French West Indies, Cuba and Haiti. Although of lesser quality, they are still worth sampling at your hotel bar. The bartender will undoubtedly be able to suggest the best local rums to you.

### Tequila

Tequila takes its name from a town in the state of Jalisco where much of it is produced. It is beyond a doubt the national drink of Mexico, and is produced by fermenting and then distilling the crushed roots from a type of agave. One traditional way of drinking tequila is to prepare lime wedges and to pour a bit of salt into the space between the thumb and the index finger of one hand. Lick the salt, swallow the tequila in a single gulp, and then bite into a lime wedge.

Tequila is also used to prepare various cocktails, especially *margaritas*.

Noteworthy among the major brands of tequila are Sauza, Hornitos, Pierro, Casa Grande, Cuervo Especial, Cuervo Gold and Orendain, all of which being the most popular with connoisseurs.

To know more about tequila, its history, manufacturing and characteristics, you must visit **Aquí es Xalisco** *(Etziquio Corona no. 303, Pitillal, ☎4-96-74, ⇌1-53-35)*, where a replica of a hand-made distillery has been built; more than 90 kinds of tequila are bottled here. **La Casa del Tequila** *(Morelos no. 589,*

*Agave*

*between Calles Corona and Aldama)* is a bar whose specialty is to serve several major brands of tequila.

---

## Eating Well

---

Too many foreign visitors to Mexico, have only a vague idea of what authentic Mexican cooking is all about. One problem is that North America has a great abundance of "Mexican" fast-food restaurants mostly offering humdrum dishes whose main connection to Mexico lies in the names they are given. These culinary dives, a real scourge for gourmets, tend to be so disrespectful of tradition that they pretentiously label themselves as Tex-Mex. North of the border, many Americans think that South American *fajitas* or Texan *chili con carne* are typical Mexican dishes. Another affront to Mexican cuisine is a dish called *nachos*, which are nothing but tortilla chips with melted cheese. What can be said for dried-out *tacos*, produced on an assembly line and shaped so that they can be piled into cardboard packaging – which is what they end up tasting like! Fortunately, it is not this sort of dish that visitors will be offered in Mexico.

Mexican cuisine varies from one part of the country to another. So, it really makes more sense to speak of regional traditions. Climatic conditions, whether in the mountains or in arid zones or by the sea, determine what local items go into the food that people eat. In Puerto Vallarta, on the Pacific coast, or on the other side of the country on the Gulf of Mexico, seafood and fish specialties are a good choice.

---

### MEXICAN RECIPES

---

### Thousand-Year-Old Traditions and Sun Cuisine in Mexico

---

Culinary art in Mexico is more than a thousand years old. Some of the dishes on the following menu are traditional, while others are innovative. Together they reveal just a tiny fragment of what Mexican cuisine has to offer. These recipes come from the renowned young chefs in Puerto Vallarta mentioned above, and all of them are easy to prepare.

PORTRAIT

**MEXICAN MENU**
**from the best restaurants in Puerto Vallarta**
(for 4 people)

*Margarita* (1)
\* \* \* \* \* \*

*Sopa de pollo con cilantro* (1)
Chicken soup with coriander
\* \* \* \* \* \*

*Guacamole* (1)
-- or --
*Enchiladas de mariscos* (2)
Seafood enchiladas
\* \* \* \* \* \*

*Filete de huachinango al chile, limón y tequila* (3)
Filet of red snapper with hot pepper,
lemon and tequila
-- or --
*Chuletas de cordero y sope mexicano* (4)
Lamb chops and seasoned cornmeal patty
\* \* \* \* \* \*

*Maiz con chorizo* (1)
Corn with sausage
\* \* \* \* \* \*

*Chocolate crème brûlée* (4)
\* \* \* \* \* \*

(1) These recipes come from the Café de Olla.
(2) One of the many specialties of La Palapa restaurant.
(3) A delightful creation by Chef Roger Dreier of the Chez Roger restaurant.
(4) This original creation comes compliments of Chef Thierry Blouet of the Café des Artistes.

---

The Recipes

---

**MARGARITA**

Makes one serving
Preparation time: 2 minutes

Tequila is a liquor made from the distilled sap of the *agave* cactus. Salt and lemon juice are important in preparing *margaritas*. At the Café de Olla, they are served with crushed ice.

Fill a shot glass:
3/4 with tequila
1/4 with orange liqueur such as Cointreau or Triple Sec
Juice of 1/2 lime
1 lime wedge
Lime zests
Salt
Finely crushed ice

Pour the tequila, the orange liqueur and the lime juice in a cocktail shaker and shake for 1 minute. Moisten the rim of the glass with the lime wedge. Put some salt in a saucer and coat the rim of the glass with it. Pour the crushed ice and then the cocktail into the glass. Garnish with a lime zest.

## CHICKEN SOUP WITH CORIANDER

Preparation time: 20 minutes
Cooking time: 1.5 hours

NOTE: In Mexico, coriander is used to season nearly all dishes and hot pepper adds extra flavour. Legumes are an important part of Mexican cuisine; black beans, for example, are used in many dishes and are often served on the side in the form of a purée, frequently with rice.

2 litres (8 cups) spring water
1 chicken breast
1 onion, finely chopped
2 garlic cloves, finely chopped
4 carrots, peeled and diced
1 bay leaf
1/2 *jalapeño* pepper, seeded and diced
125 ml (1/2 cup) rice
125 ml (1/2 cup) chick peas, cooked and drained
65 ml (1/4 cup) fresh coriander finely chopped
Juice of 1 lime
Salt to taste

PORTRAIT

Pour the water into a pot. Add the chicken, onion, garlic, carrots, bay leaf and *jalapeño* pepper. Allow to simmer for one hour. Take out the chicken, remove its skin and bones, then cut it into small pieces and set it aside.

Skim the fat off the broth. Add the rice, and let simmer for twenty minutes. Add the chick peas, coriander and lime juice and salt to taste. Let simmer for another 10 minutes. May be served with *guacamole* tacos (see recipe below).


## GUACAMOLE

Preparation time: 15 minutes

SUGGESTION: serve the *guacamole* with warm tortillas or tacos.

4 avocados, pitted and peeled
30 ml (2 tbsp) lime juice
1 onion, finely chopped
1 fresh green hot pepper, sliced lengthwise, seeded and chopped
15 ml (1 tbsp) fresh coriander, finely chopped
2 tomatoes, peeled and cut into small cubes
Salt to taste
Lettuce leaves

Beat the avocado into a smooth purée. Pour the lime juice over it, and mix while adding the onion, hot pepper and coriander. Add tomato and salt and mix again. Lay out the lettuce leaves and place the *guacamole* on top.


## SEAFOOD ENCHILADAS

Makes 12 *enchiladas* (3 to 4 servings)
Preparation time: 30 minutes
Time for the tortilla dough to sit: 45 minutes
Cooking time: 30 minutes

**Tortillas**
500 ml (2 cups) corn flour
5 ml (1 tsp) salt

300 ml (1 ¼ cups) boiling water
Vegetable oil

**Fillings and sauce**
375 g (3/4 lb) scallops
375 g (3/4 lb) small shrimps
125 ml (1/2 cup) fish stock
65 ml (1/4 cup) dry white wine
125 ml (1/2 cup) thick white *béchamel* sauce
Tabasco sauce to taste
250 g (1/2 lb) grated *gruyère* cheese
65 ml (1/4 cup) heavy cream (35%)
65 ml (1/4 cup) fresh coriander, finely chopped
Salt and ground black pepper to taste
Avocado slices for garnish
Juice of 1/2 lime
1 tomato, cut into small cubes

Mix the flour and salt in a bowl, shape into a mound, making a well in the centre of the mound. Gradually pour the boiling water into the well and knead it until you have a ball of dough. Cover the bowl with a dry cloth and let rest for 30 minutes at room temperature.

Dust a small work area and a rolling pin lightly with flour. Take a piece of dough about the size of a small egg and shape it into a thin pancake about 15 cm (6 inches) across. Repeat this process, and keep the pancakes between sheets of waxed paper.

Lightly grease a saucepan. Heat the pan and cook the pancakes (tortillas) for about 2 minutes on each side. Keep them warm by separating them with aluminum foil.

Poach the scallops and shrimps for 3 minutes in the fish stock and white wine, shaking them lightly and then setting them aside. Warm the *béchamel* sauce, spiked with Tabasco, then blend in the seafood, fish stock and cheese, mixing until smooth. Remove from the heat, add cream and coriander, and season to taste.

Coat the tortillas with the seafood and the sauce, browning lightly for 5 minutes in the oven. Place the *enchiladas* on a warm serving dish. Garnish with avocado slices sprinkled with lime juice, tomato and fresh coriander.

## FILLET OF RED SNAPPER WITH HOT PEPPER, LEMON AND TEQUILA

Preparation time: 15 minutes
Cooking time: about 10 minutes

Frying was introduced by the Spanish to Mexico, where many foods are now prepared this way. Snapper can be replaced with sole, cod or plaice. Serve this dish with potatoes *au gratin* or with a Mexican-style polenta (see recipe below) and a green vegetable of your choice.

**Fish**
825 g (1 ¾ lbs) fish fillets (4 fillets)
Salt and ground black pepper to taste
375 ml (3/4 cup) dried bread crumbs
45 ml (3 tbsp) crushed dried hot pepper
125 g (1/4 lb) butter
Fresh coriander, for garnish
2 limes, cut in quarters, for garnish
Slices of marinated red bell pepper

**Sauce**
375 ml (3/4 cup) dry white wine
2 egg yolks
65 ml (1/4 cup) heavy cream (35%)
65 ml (1/4 cup) tequila
45 ml (3 tbsp) lime juice
Salt and ground black pepper to taste

Sprinkle salt and pepper on the fish fillets. Melt half the butter and baste one side of the fillets, then sprinkle the same side with bread crumbs and dried hot pepper, pressing with the palm of the hand to make mixture stick to the fish. Heat a saucepan and add the rest of the butter. Cook the fillets for 2 minutes on the seasoned side and then turn them gently to the other side, allowing them to cook 2 minutes longer. Prepare the sauce while keeping them warm.

PORTRAIT

Reduce the wine to half its volume in a saucepan. Whip egg yolks and cream, then add to the wine. Pour in tequila and lime juice, add salt and pepper, and mix.

Lay the fillets, seasoned side up, on a warm serving dish, and pour the sauce around them. Decorate the serving dish with sprigs of coriander, lime wedges and bell pepper slices.

## LAMB CHOPS AND MEXICAN POLENTA

Preparation time: 30 minutes
Cooking time: about 20 minutes

NOTE: Lamb tender loin can be found in the meat section of many food stores. Ask the butcher to trim the loins for you. As an alternative, you may choose lamb chops, with 3 per person.

### Meat
4 servings loin of lamb, or 3 lamb chops per person
30 ml (2 tbsp) chili sauce
30 ml (2 tbsp) roasted sesame seeds

### Polenta
250 ml (1 cup) corn flour
250 ml (1 cup) water
125 g (1/4 lb) grated strong cheddar
Cumin to taste
15 ml (1 tbsp) wheat flour
Salt and ground black pepper to taste

### Sauce
250 ml (1 cup) lamb, beef or veal broth
Dried hot pepper to taste
1 garlic clove, finely chopped
1 small onion, finely chopped
30 ml (2 tbsp) vinegar
A few cumin seeds
1 pinch thyme
1 bay leaf
Salt and ground black pepper to taste
30 ml (1 tbsp) butter

PORTRAIT

Sprinkle lamb with salt and pepper, bake it in the oven for 6 minutes at 250° C (475° F.). Baste with a little chili sauce, and sprinkle with sesame seeds.

Mix corn flour and water, then knead to obtain a slightly sticky dough. Add cheese, cumin and wheat flour. Cut dough into four pieces, flattening them into circles 15 cm (6 inches) across. Cook in a dry saucepan for 5 minutes on each side, turning once so that they are slightly grilled. Wrap them in a towel and set aside.

Heat broth and reduce to half its volume, adding the hot pepper, garlic, onion, vinegar, cumin and herbs. Remove from the heat, add salt and pepper, then whip in the butter. Place one cornmeal patty in the centre of each plate, laying the lamb on top and coating it with sauce. Serve immediately.

## CORN WITH SAUSAGE

Preparation time: 5 minutes
Cooking time: 10 minutes

SUGGESTION: The original recipe calls for *chorizo*, a type of sausage quite common in Mexico, but bacon strips can be used instead, and the *jalapeño* pepper can be replaced with Tabasco sauce. *Chorizo* is a medium-sized sausage sold fresh or dried in some Spanish and Latin American food shops.

1/2 link spicy *chorizo*, cut into small cubes
30 ml (2 tbsp) sunflower or corn oil
1 onion, finely chopped
1 red bell pepper, cut into tiny pieces
1 green bell pepper, cut into tiny pieces
2 peeled tomatoes
500 ml (2 cups) corn, drained
1/2 *jalapeño* pepper, seeded and cut into strips
60 ml (4 tbsp) fresh coriander, finely chopped
Salt to taste

Brown the *chorizo* in hot oil on the stove, adding the onion, bell peppers, tomatoes, corn and hot pepper. Cook uncovered for about 10 minutes, then add coriander and salt.

## CHOCOLATE CRÈME BRÛLÉE

Serves 12
Preparation time: 20 minutes
Cooking time: about 10 minutes
Refrigeration time: 3 hours

NOTE: *Crème brûlée* is a type of custard with a hard coating. Chocolate is a favourite in Mexico, the birthplace of cacao. Mexicans even use chocolate in certain spicy dishes, the best known of which is *mole poblano de guajolate*, turkey simmered in a sauce made of bitter chocolate and hot peppers.

The following recipe makes a lot, but *crème brûlée* keeps well for a few days, and your guests will certainly want seconds.

1 litre (4 cups) sour cream
12 egg yolks
5 ml (1 tsp) sugar
15 ml (1 tbsp) cornstarch
15 ml (1 tbsp) vanilla extract
15 ml (1 tbsp) white rum
250 g (1/2 lb) sweetened chocolate
500 ml (2 cups) sugar
45 ml (3 tbsp) spring water

Warm sour cream and set aside. Beat egg yolks and sugar, along with cornstarch, vanilla and rum, then add this mixture to the sour cream. Melt chocolate over low heat, then blend into mixture. Bring mixture to a boil over low heat, stirring with a wooden spoon. Pour into cups or ramekins and refrigerate for 3 hours.

Heat the 2 cups of sugar and water in a pot until it turns golden brown, then pour it carefully (don't burn yourself!) over each of the cooled creams. Allow to harden before serving.

## PRACTICAL INFORMATION

**T**his section is intended to help you plan your trip to Puerto Vallarta and to other destinations in Mexico. The State of Jalisco, on the Pacific coast, is home to Puerto Vallarta, a choice destination in the grand Bahía Banderas (Bay of Flags) that is worth carefully planning for. In addition to invaluable advice, this chapter provides practical suggestions so visitors can familiarize themselves with Mexico's fabulous one-thousand-year old culture and traditions.

---

ENTRANCE FORMALITIES

---

Passport

---

To enter Mexico, you must have a valid passport. This is by far the most widely accepted piece of identification, and therefore the safest. As a general rule, the expiration date should not fall less than three months after your date of departure. If you have a return ticket, however, your passport need only be valid for the duration of your stay. If not, proof of sufficient funds may be required. For travellers from most Western countries (Canada, United States, Australia, New Zealand, Western European countries) a simple passport is enough, no visa is necessary. Other citizens are advised to contact the nearest consulate to see if they need a visa to enter. Since requirements for entering the country can change quickly, it is wise to double-check them before leaving.

Travellers are advised to keep a photocopy of the most important pages of their passport, as well as to write down its number and date of issue. If ever this document is lost or stolen, this will facilitate the replacement process. In case of such an event, contact your country's embassy or consulate (see addresses below) in order to be reissued an equivalent document as soon as possible.

## Minors Entering the Country

In Mexico, all individuals under 18 years of age are legally considered minors. Each traveller under the age of 18 is therefore required to present written proof of his or her status upon entering the country, namely, a letter of consent signed by his or her parents or legal guardians and notarized or certified by a representative of the court (a justice of the peace or a commissioner for oaths).

A minor accompanied by only one parent must carry a signed letter of consent from the other parent, which also must be notarized or certified by a representative of the court.

If the minor has only one legally recognized parent, he or she must have a paper attesting to that fact. Again, this document must be notarized or certified by a justice of the peace of a commissioner for oaths.

Airline companies require adults who are meeting minors unaccompanied by their parents or an official guardian to provide their address and telephone number.

## Student and Business Visas

Students and businesspeople wishing to reside in Mexico for a certain period of time should request information from the

Mexican embassies and consulates in their home country (see addresses below).

## Customs

On the way to Mexico, the flight attendants will hand out a questionnaire to all air passengers; this is a customs declaration form, which must be completed before your arrival. You will be requested to fill in your name and address and indicate where you will be staying in Mexico. You must also declare any personal belongings valued at over $1,000 US that you are bringing into the country.

In addition to clothing and other personal effects, travellers over 18 are allowed to bring in 3 l of wine or spirits, 400 cigarettes or two boxes of cigars, a reasonable amount of perfume or toilet water for personal use and a maximum of 12 rolls of film for their camera; the total value of these items must not exceed $300 US. Of course, it is strictly forbidden to bring any drugs or firearms into the country. All personal medication, especially psychotropic drugs, must have a prescription label on them.

At customs in Puerto Vallarta's international airport, a green light means you are free to go and a red light means you must undergo a standard search.

## Tourist Cards

Upon your arrival in Mexico, after your proof of citizenship and customs declaration form have been checked, the customs officer will give you a blue tourist card. This card is free and authorizes its holder to visit the country. Make sure not to lose it, as you must return it to Mexican immigration when you leave the country. Take the same precautions as you would with your passport, by recording the tourist card number somewhere else — on your airline ticket, for example.

Should you lose your tourist card, head to the immigration office. Your card will be replaced, but you must prove how and when you entered the country (a plane ticket will do).

## Airport Departure Tax

Except for children under two years of age, all passengers taking international flights out of Mexico are required to pay a tax of about $12 US. The major airlines often include this tax in the ticket price; ask your travel agent.

## EMBASSIES AND CONSULATES

Embassies and consulates can provide precious information to visitors who find themselves in a difficult situation (for example, in the event of an accident or death, they can provide names of doctors, lawyers, etc.). They deal only with urgent cases, however. It should be noted that costs arising from such services are not paid by these consular missions.

## Foreign Embassies and Consulates in Mexico

Here are a few addresses of embassies in the federal capital Mexico City, and consulates in the capital of the State of Jalisco, Guadalajara, and in Puerto Vallarta.

**Australia**
Australian Embassy
Ruben Darío 55
Col. Polanco
11560 - Mexico D.F.
☎(5) 531-5225
⊶(5) 203-8431

**Belgium**
Belgian Embassy
Avenida Alfredo de Musset, n° 41
Colonia Polanco
11550 - Mexico, D.F.
☎(5) 280-0758
⊶(5) 280-0208

**Canada**
Canadian Embassy
Calle Schiller, n° 529
(Rincón del Bosque)
Colonia Polanco
11560 - Mexico, D.F.
☎(5) 254-3288
⊶(5) 254-8554

Canadian Consulate
Hôtel Fiesta Americana
Office 30-A
Calle Aurelio Aceves, n° 225
Sector Juárez
44100 - Guadalajara (Jalisco)
☎(3) 825-3434 ext. 3005

Canadian Consulate
Ms. Lyne Benoit
Calle Hidalgo, n°160
Office 10
Colonia Centro 48300
Puerto Vallarta (Jalisco)
☎(322) 2-53-98
⚏(322) 3-08-58
benoit@canada.org.mx

**Germany**
German Honourary Consulate
Casa Wagner de Guadalajara
S.A.D.C.V.
Avenida Ramon Corona 202
Guadalajara, JAL
☎613-1414
⚏613-2609

**Great Britain**
British Embassy
Lerma 71
Col. Cuauhtémoc
06500 Mexico D.F.
☎(525) 207-2089
⚏(525) 207-7672

**Italy**
Italian Embassy
Avenida Paseo de las Palmas,
n° 1994
11000 - Mexico, D.F.
☎(5) 596-3655
⚏(5) 596-7710

**Spain**
Spanish Embassy
Galileo, n° 114
Colonia Polanco
11560 - Mexico, D.F.
☎(5) 596-3655
⚏(5) 596-7710

**Switzerland**
Swiss Embassy
Torre Optima, 11. Stock,
Avenida Paseo de las Palmas,
n° 405
Lomas de Chapltepec
11000 - Mexico, D.F.
☎(5) 520-8535 or
(5) 520-3003
⚏(5) 520-8685

**United States**
American Embassy
Passeo de la Reforma,
n° 1305
06500 - Mexico, D.F.
☎(5) 211-0042
⚏(5) 511-9980

American Consulate
Zaragoza n° 160
Edificio Vallarta Plaza
Office 18, Puerto Vallarta
(Jalisco)
☎(322) 2-00-69 or
(322) 2-00-74
⚏(3) 826-6549

PRACTICAL
INFORMATION

## Mexican Embassies and Consulates Abroad

**Australia**
Mexican Embassy
14 Perth Avenue
Yarratumla, ACT 2600
☎(02) 6273-3963,
6273-3905 or 6273-3947,
⇎(02) 6273-1190

**Belgium**
Mexican Embassy
164, chaussée de la Hulpe
1st floor
1170 - Bruxelles
☎(32-2) 676-0711
⇎(32-2) 676-9312

**Canada**
Mexican Embassy
45 O'Connor Street
Office 1500, Ottawa, Ont.
K1P 1A4
☎(613) 233-8988 or
233-9572
⇎(613) 235-9123

Consulate General of Mexico
2000, rue Mansfield
Suite 1015
Montréal (Québec)
H3A 2Z7
☎(514) 288-2502
⇎(514) 288-8287

Consulate General of Mexico
Commerce Court West
99 Bay Street
Toronto, Ont.
M5L 1E9
☎(416) 368-2875
⇎(416) 368-3478

**Germany**
Mexican Embassy
Adenauerallee 100
53113 Bonn
☎(0228) 914860

**Great Britain**
Mexican Embassy
8 Halkin Street
London SWIX 7DW
☎(0171) 235-6393,
⇎(0171) 235-5480

**Switzerland**
Mexican Embassy
Bernastrasse, n° 57
3005 - Berne
☎(031) 351-1875
⇎(031) 351-3492
Note: there are honourary consulates of Mexico in Zurich and Lausanne; their addresses are available from the embassy in Berne.

**United States**
Mexican Embassy
1911 Pennsylvania Avenue, N.W.
20006 - Washington D.C.
☎(202) 728-1633
⇎(202) 728-1698

Mexican Consulate
27 East 39th Street
New York, N.Y.
10016
☎(212) 217-6400,
⇎(212) 217-6493

# TOURIST INFORMATION

## Mexican Tourist Associations Abroad

**North America**
Mexico Hotline
☎(800) 44-MEXICO or
(800) 446-3942

**Canada**
1 Place Ville-Marie
Suite 1931
Montréal (Québec)
H3B 2C3
☎(514) 871-1052
≈(514) 871-3825

2 Bloor Street West
Office 1801
Toronto, Ont.
M4W 3E2
☎(416) 925-0704
≈(416) 925-6061

**Germany**
Wiesenhuettenplatz 26
60329 Frankfurt-am-Main 1
☎496-925-2413
≈496-925-3755

**Great Britain**
60-61 Trafalgar Square
London WC2N 5DS
☎(44-171) 734-1058
≈(44-171) 930-9202

**Italy**
Via Barberini 3, 7o. Piso
Rome 00187
☎(39-06) 487-2182/4698
≈(39-06) 48-3630

**Spain**
Calle Velázquez, no. 126
Madrid 28006
☎(34-91) 561-3520
≈(34-91) 411-0759

**United States**
21 East 63rd Street
Third floor
New York, N.Y.
10021
☎(212) 821-0313
≈(212) 821-0367

2401 West 6th Street
Fifth floor
Los Angeles, CA
90057
☎(213) 351-2069 or
351-2075/76
≈(213) 351-2074

PRACTICAL
INFORMATION

Tourist Associations in Mexico

**Puerto Vallarta**

Secretaria de Turismo del Estado de Jalisco
Dirección Regional de Turismo en Puerto Vallarta:
Juárez e Independencia
Planta Baja Palacio Municipal
☎91 (322) 2-02-42, 3-07-44 or 3-08-44
≈91 (322) 2-02-43
B.P. 48300 Puerto Vallarta, Jalisco, México
*(Mon to Fri 9am to 7pm, Sat and Sun 9am to 1pm)*

**State of Jalisco**

Morelos, n° 102
Plaza Tapatía
Guadalajara (Jalisco)
México
B.P. 44100
☎614-86-86 or 613-0359, ≈613-0335
Tourist information for the state of Jalisco:
Toll free numbers in Mexico, ☎(800) 363-22 or 658-22-22

**Bahía of Banderas and the State of Narayit**

The tourist information booth for the Bahía de Banderas and the state of Nayarit is a few kilometres after Bucerias, at the intersection with Highway 200.

Delegación de Turismo de Bahía de Banderas y Nayarit
Bucerias
☎(329) 8-00-49
≈(329) 8-04-15

Presidencia Municipal de Bahía de Banderas
Valle de Banderas (Nayarit)
☎(329) 1-00-35, 1-02-65 or 1-03-50

Secretaría de Turismo (Nayarit)
Avenidad de la Cultura no. 74
Ciúdad del Valle
Tepic (Nayarit)
☎(32) 14-80-71 or 14-80-73
⇌(32) 14-80-74

---

## EXCURSIONS AND GUIDED TOURS

The possibilities for excursions in and around Puerto Vallarta are endless. Stands line the sidewalks in town offering all manner of activities (boat trips, mountain-bike rentals, hotel tours, etc.); people may even try to sell you a time-share property after a short, simple conversation. If you plan on visiting the parks and natural areas, it is a good idea to seek out the services of a serious, reputable company. See the "Outdoors" chapter for a list of some agencies classified according to activity.

### Tour Agencies

Roberto Bravo
Viajes Paraíso
Plaza Flamingos
Avenida México, n° 1082
Suite 303
☎2-03-90 or 4-32-70
⇌3-20-24

---

## SPANISH COURSES

Instituto Técnico Vallarta
Francisco Medina Ascencio n° 1037
☎3-22-08

Colonia 5 de Diciembre
C.P. 48350
☎2-03-90 or 4-32-70
⇌3-20-24

Roberto Bravo
Plaza Flamingos
Avenida México, n° 1082
Suite 303
Colonia 5 de Diciembre C.P. 48350
☎2-03-90 or 4-32-70
⇆3-20-24

## ENTERING THE COUNTRY

### By Plane

**From Canada**

There are several (up to four per week in the winter) direct flights from Toronto, Montreal and Vancouver to Mexico City with Canadian Airlines (☎800-661-8881) or Mexicana (800-531-7923, www.mexicana.com). Your options increase considerably if you take a charter flight. Canada 3000 and Air Transat (☎514-476-1118) offer such direct flights to Puerto Vallarta; these can be arranged via your travel agent and are often part of package deals which include accommodations, airfare and transfers. Canadian travellers can also travel through a United States' gateway city (see below).

**From the United States**

Continental Airlines, Delta Airlines, American Airlines, Mexicana and AeroMéxico (☎800-237-6639) fly out of a handful of U.S. gateway cities directly to Puerto Vallarta. These cities include Houston, San Francisco, Los Angeles, Dallas, Miami and Chicago. Most of the major carriers fly to Mexico City, from which connector flights to Puerto Vallarta or Guadalajara are numerous.

**From Europe**

KLM and British Airways have flights to Mexico City from Amsterdam and London, respectively. Once in the capital connector flights are plentiful.

## Gustavo Díaz Ordaz International Airport

Gustavo Díaz Ordaz International Airport *(Carreta a Tepic, km 7.5, ☎1-13-25)*, Puerto Vallarta's international airport, located 7.5 kilometres from downtown, has two terminals. The first is for domestic and international arrivals. When you go through customs, you will be asked to press a button to turn on a green light, which means that you can enter the country with no further ado, or a red light, which means that you will have to be searched first.

The second terminal is for departures, and it is there that you will find postal services, duty-free shops (which often have higher prices than downtown stores) and a newsstand with a good choice of books by Latin American authors, as well as a few current American bestsellers. This terminal also contains a small snack bar, several car-rental agencies and a currency exchange office.

**Getting Downtown from the Airport**

It takes about 20 minutes to get from the airport to downtown Puerto Vallarta by car or by bus *(camión)*. Given the risk of theft, the shuttle traffic and the fact that you will be lugging your baggage around, the most convenient option by far is to take a taxi. The fare is determined according to how many zones you pass through, so the trip downtown should cost no more than 70 pesos. Purchase a taxi ticket at the stand at the airport exit, then give it to the driver; no further payment is required, unless you have a lot of baggage, in which case a tip is in order. Take note that the taxi ride is included in most vacation packages offered by travel agencies.

PRACTICAL INFORMATION

## Airline Companies in Puerto Vallarta

Aéro Mexico
☎4-27-77

Air Transat
☎2-38-83

Canadian International and Canadian Holidays
☎1-12-12

Continental Airlines (Air Canada affiliate)
☎1-10-25 or 1-10-96

Mexicana
☎4-97-96

## INSURANCE

### Cancellation Insurance

Your travel agent will usually offer you cancellation insurance upon purchase of your airline ticket or vacation package. This insurance allows you to be reimbursed for the ticket or package deal if your trip must be cancelled due to serious illness or death. Healthy people are unlikely to need this protection, which is therefore only of relative use.

### Theft Insurance

Most residential insurance policies protect some of your goods from theft, even if the theft occurs in a foreign country. To make a claim, you must fill out a police report. Usually the coverage for a theft abroad is 10% of your total coverage. It may not be necessary to take out further insurance, depending on the amount covered by your current policy. As policies vary considerably, you are advised to check with your insurance company. European visitors should take out baggage insurance.

## Life Insurance

Several airline companies offer a life insurance plan included in the price of the airplane ticket. However, many travellers already have this type of insurance and do not require additional coverage.

## Health Insurance

Health insurance is without question the most useful kind of insurance for travellers. It should be purchased before setting off on a trip. The insurance policy should be as comprehensive as possible, because health care costs add up quickly, even in Mexico. When purchasing the policy, make sure it covers medical expenses of all kinds, such as hospitalization, nursing services and doctor's fees (at fairly high rates, as these are expensive). A repatriation clause, in case necessary care cannot be administered on site, is invaluable. In addition, you may have to pay upon leaving the clinic, so you should check your policy to see what provisions it includes for such instances. During your stay in Mexico, you should always keep proof that you are insured on your person to avoid any confusion in case of an accident.

**PRACTICAL INFORMATION**

## HEALTH

Mexico is a wonderful country to visit. Unfortunately, travellers do run the risk of contracting certain diseases there, such as malaria, typhoid, diphtheria, tetanus, polio and hepatitis A and B. Though such cases are rare they do occur. When planning your trip, therefore, consult your doctor (or a clinic for travellers) about what precautions to take. Don't forget that preventing these illnesses is easier than curing them. It is therefore practical to take medications, vaccines and necessary precautions in order to avoid medical problems likely to become serious. If, however, you do have to see a doctor, keep in mind that it will cost about 100 Pesos (about $15 US) per visit. In such cases, local agents working for foreign tour operators (mainly in big hotels) can help you find one. Another option is to contact the IAMAT (International Association for Medical

Assistance to Travellers) in Puerto Vallarta. The members of this organization are qualified doctors, and most speak several languages, including English. A consultation at one of their clinics costs $50 US. Puerto Vallarta has a number of reputable hospitals as well (see p 60).

## Illnesses

Cases of hepatitis A and B, AIDS and certain venereal diseases have been reported in Mexico, so it is wise to take necessary precautions.

Bodies of fresh water are often contaminated with the bacteria that causes schistosomiasis. This illness results when a parasite invades the body and attacks the liver and nervous system, and it is difficult to treat. Swimming in fresh water should therefore be avoided.

Remember that excessive alcohol intake can cause dehydration and illness, especially when accompanied by lengthy exposure to the sun.

Because medical facilities are sometimes rudimentary, make sure (if possible) that quality control tests have been properly carried out before any blood transfusion.

Although the tap water in Puerto Vallarta has been declared potable by the Ministry of Health, visitors are strongly advised to drink purified water only. This goes for all of Mexico. Puerto Vallarta's water supply comes from a stream in Mismaloya and is treated by the Seapal company *(information, ☎322-3-11-80)*.

The medical problems travellers are most likely to encounter are usually a result of poorly treated water containing bacteria that cause upset stomach, diarrhea or fever. To avoid this risk, drink only bottled water, which is available just about all over the country. When buying a bottle, whether in a restaurant or a store, always make sure that it is well sealed. In large hotels, water is usually treated, but you should always double-check with the staff before drinking any. Fruit and vegetables rinsed in tap water (those not peeled before eating) can cause the same problems. Visitors should be doubly careful in low budget restaurants, which do not always have the equipment necessary to ensure proper hygiene. The same goes for the small street vendors as well as those on the beach (be particularly careful with brochettes and grilled fish). Finally, dairy products are perfectly safe for consumption in Puerto Vallarta.

If you do get diarrhea, there are several methods of treating it. Try to soothe your digestive system by avoiding solids and drinking carbonated beverages, tea or coffee (with no milk) until your symptoms lessen. Drink a lot of liquids to avoid dehydration, which can be dangerous. To remedy severe dehydration, drink a solution made up of one litre (4 cups) of water, three teaspoons of salt and one teaspoon of sugar. You can also find ready-made preparations in most pharmacies; for example, Pedialyte is available in several flavours: natural, cherry, strawberry or coconut (this last one is the best choice). Next, gradually start reintroducing solids to your diet by eating foods that are easy to digest. Medications like Imodium, Pepto Bismol or Lomotil can help control an upset stomach. These are available in most pharmacies in Puerto Vallarta and throughout Mexico. They can, however, cause severe constipation which can allow certain bacteria to enter the bloodstream. If your symptoms persist and are severe (high fever, violent diarrhea), you may need antibiotics, in which case it is best to consult a doctor. If possible, avoid injections and take only oral medication.

Food and climate can also cause various health problems. Make sure that food is fresh (especially fish and meat) and that the area in which it is prepared is clean. Proper hygiene, such as washing hands frequently, will also help keep you healthy.

PRACTICAL INFORMATION

## Insects

Insects are found in great numbers all over the country and can often be very unpleasant. They are particularly numerous during the rainy season. Nevertheless, in order to avoid being eaten alive, cover up well in the evening (when insects are most active), avoid perfume and brightly coloured clothing and arm yourself with a good insect repellant. Shoes and socks that protect your feet and legs are very practical for walking in the forest or mountains. It is also advisable to bring along ointment to relieve the irritation in case you do get bitten.

Scorpions are a real nuisance, especially during the dry season, and their bites can cause high fevers, or even prove fatal to someone in a fragile state of health. Scorpions have the annoying habit of creeping into houses and other buildings on the ground floor. It is therefore necessary to take a few precautions. Avoid leaving your shoes on the ground. Check out all the nooks and crannies in public bathrooms, and use a flashlight so you can see clearly when you're walking after dark. If you take a nap on a hammock or on a chaise longue, make sure to shake it out well before lying down on it. Anyone who gets bitten by a scorpion should be taken to a doctor or a hospital immediately. The same measures apply to snake bites.

## The Sun

Despite its benefits, the sun also causes numerous problems. Always use sunblock to protect yourself from the sun's harmful rays. Many of the sunscreens on the market do not provide adequate protection. Before setting off on your trip, ask your pharmacist which ones are truly effective against the danger-ous rays of the sun. For the best results, apply the cream at least 20 minutes before going out in the sun. Overexposure to the sun can cause sunstroke, symptoms of which include dizziness, vomiting and fever. It is important to keep well protected and avoid prolonged exposure, especially during the first few days of your trip, as it takes a while to get used to the sun's strength. Even after a few days, moderate exposure is best. A hat and pair of sunglasses are indispensable accessories in this part of the world.

## Hospitals

CMQ Hospital
Basilio Badillo
*(south of Río Cuale, on the corner of Calle Insurgentes)*
☎2-35-72

## Useful Phone Numbers

The area code for Puerto Vallarta is **322**.

Police: ☎2-01-23 or 2-01-06
Red Cross: ☎2-15-33
Canadian Consulate: ☎2-53-98
American Consulate: ☎2-00-69
Airport: ☎1-13-25
Port (Terminal Maritima): ☎4-04-27
Alcoholics Anonymous: ☎2-18-78 or 2-55-88

Medasist Hospital
24 hours
Manuel M. Deguez, n° 360
*(south of Río Cuale, near Calle Insurgentes, south of Calle Basilio Badillo)*
☎3-04-44 or 2-33-01

AMERIMED
American Medical Clinic
24 hours
Plaza Neptune, Marina Vallarta
*(at the marina entrance)*
☎1-00-23 or 1-00-24
≈1-00-26

Pharmacies

CMQ Pharmacy
Candelaria 101 and
Basilio Badillo
*(on the corner of la Calle Insurgentes, open 24 hours a day)*
☎2-29-41 or 2-13-30

CLIMATE

Starting beyond the western side of the Sierra Madre del Sur, which faces the Pacific coast, is a region with tropical temperatures that vary little year-round; the average temperature is 22°C. This is the climate enjoyed by Puerto Vallarta, where the days are hot and the nights comfortable, except during the rainy season.

The temperature is not the same everywhere. The state of Jalisco actually has four fairly distinct climatic zones, which vary according to altitude and geographic location. Puerto Vallarta lies in a climatic zone that starts to the northwest and extends in a vast strip between the mountains and the sea to the southern end of the state of Jalisco, whose border with the state of Colima is marked by the Río Cihuatlan. This is not the largest climatic zone in the state. East of the Sierra Madre del Sur, a semitropical climate reigns over three-quarters of Jalisco. The average annual temperatures there range from 18°C to 22°C. The two other climatic zones, temperate (from 12°C to 18°C) and semi-temperate (from 5°C to 18°C), exist in distinct microcosms throughout the territory.

In the early days of colonization, the Spanish realized that the regions located at high altitudes enjoyed the most comfortable climates and were therefore best suited to establishing new communities. This was an observation, not a discovery, for the Aztecs had already built the imperial city of Tenochtitlán (Mexico City) over 2,000 m above sea level, thus protecting its inhabitants from the torrid climate found in many other parts of the country. Mexico City, like Guadalajara, the capital of the state of Jalisco, enjoys an almost ideal climate, with an average temperature of about 18.3°C.

The seaside city of Puerto Vallarta thus boasts a unique setting and, from November to May, a relatively unvarying tropical climate. During this part of the year, from autumn to spring, the days are hot but dry enough to be tolerable, and the nights are wonderfully mild. The rainy season lasts from June to October, and is marked by violent downpours, with the rainfall reaching up to 27.6 cm during July and 28.8 cm in August and September. It is also humid here during these months.

The following is a list of the average temperatures in Celsius (°C), as well as the average rainfall in centimetres (cm) for the regions of Puerto Vallarta and Guadalajara, the capital of the state of Jalisco, which is located 1,592 m above sea-level and enjoys a remarkably temperate climate

## Puerto Vallarta

| Month | Temperature (°C / °F) | Precipitation (cm / in) |
|---|---|---|
| January | 22.7 / 72.8 | 1.25 / 0.5 |
| February | 22.2 / 72 | 0.62 / 0.24 |
| March | 24.4 / 75.9 | 0.62 / 0.24 |
| April | 24.4 / 75.9 | 0.62 / 0.24 |
| May | 26.6 / 79.9 | 0.62 / 0.24 |
| June | 28 / 82.4 | 15 / 5.91 |
| July | 29 / 84.2 | 27.6 / 10.8 |
| August | 29 / 84.2 | 28.8 / 11.3 |
| September | 28.8 / 83.9 | 28.8 / 11.3 |
| October | 27 / 80.6 | 30 / 11.8 |
| November | 26 / 78.8 | 28.8 / 11.3 |
| December | 25.5 / 77.9 | 25.5 / 10 |

## Guadalajara

| Month | Temperature (°C / °F) | Precipitation (cm / in) |
|---|---|---|
| January | 14.4 / 58 | 1.8 / 0.71 |
| February | 16.1 / 61 | 0.5 / 0.2 |
| March | 18.3 / 65 | 0.2 / 0.08 |
| April | 21.1 / 70 | 0.7 / 0.28 |
| May | 22.2 / 72 | 1.8 / 0.71 |
| June | 21.6 / 70.9 | 19 / 7.48 |
| July | 20.5 / 68.9 | 25 / 9.84 |
| August | 20 / 68 | 19.7 / 7.76 |
| September | 19.4 / 66.9 | 17.5 / 6.89 |
| October | 18.3 / 64.9 | 5.2 / 2.5 |
| November | 16.1 / 61 | 2 / 0.79 |
| December | 15 / 59 | 2 / 0.79 |

PRACTICAL INFORMATION

## PACKING

The type of clothing visitors should bring to Puerto Vallarta varies little from one season to the next. In general, loose, comfortable cotton clothing is most practical. For walking in the city, it is better to wear shoes that cover the entire foot, since these provide the best protection against cuts that can become infected. For cool evenings, a long-sleeved shirt or sweater can be useful. Remember to wear rubber sandals on the beach. During the rainy season, bring a small umbrella to keep dry during the showers. When visiting certain sights (churches for example), a skirt that hangs below the knees or a pair of pants should be worn, so don't forget to include the appropriate article of clothing in your suitcase. Finally, if you intend to go on an excursion in the mountains, take along a good pair of shoes and a sweater.

Plan on wearing good shoes even in the city for the streets of Puerto Vallarta are cobblestoned and sidewalks are uneven: one often encounters cracks, steps, holes and other such things. During rain showers, the streets turn into rivers carrying mud and garbage in their wake.

## SAFETY AND SECURITY

Puerto Vallarta survives on tourism, and a special police force dressed in white uniforms looks out for visitors' safety. These officers speak both Spanish and English. There are three other police forces in Puerto Vallarta as well: the municipal police, the state police, and the federal police.

Keep in mind that to the majority of Mexicans, your personal belongings (cameras, leather suitcases, video camera, jewellery, etc.) represent a great deal of money. A certain attitude and a suitable degree of cautiousness can help prevent a lot of problems. It is therefore in your best interest to wear little or no jewellery, keep your electronic equipment in a nondescript bag slung across your chest and avoid showing all your money when paying for something. You can conceal your travellers' cheques, passport and some of your cash in a money belt that fits under your clothing; this way if your bags are ever stolen you will still have the papers and money necessary to get by. Remember, the less attention you attract, the less chance you have of being robbed.

# TRANSPORTATION

## By Car

It is easy to rent a car in Puerto Vallarta. Generally speaking, the largest rental agencies are found at the airport and in certain hotels, and the lesser known ones in the northern part of town, on Paseo de las Palmas. The rates are in US dollars and vary considerably from one place to the next. For example, renting an all-terrain vehicle can cost anywhere from $35 US to $90 US. Convertibles are available for $35 US to $60 US, and pick-up trucks for less. These rates are usually for one day, including taxes, 200 km and insurance. It is very important that the insurance be included, so be insistent on that point. The roads are narrow, and the traffic can make for difficult driving. The maximum speed limit is 90 km/h on highways and 50 to 80 km/h on secondary roads, and you'll often come across police officers making speed checks.

Bear in mind that thieves are a problem here, and that many travellers have had their vehicle and all their belongings stolen. For this reason, especially because the city's main attractions are located very close to one another, we do not recommend renting a car if you are planning to spend your entire trip in Puerto Vallarta. **N.B.**: a reminder that it is a dangerous for women to drive alone, particularly in regions far from major urban centres.

### Entering Mexico by Car

Entering Mexico by car requires much patience on the part of drivers as realized by your humble authors having undertaken this journey. The generous advice offered herein is the fruit of our experience, culled first and foremost in the border cities of Laredo (Texas), US, and Nuevo Laredo (Nuevo Léon), Mexico, as well as all through a month-long trip by car throughout the country.

PRACTICAL
INFORMATION

**The Mexican-US Border**

Before taking a trip to Mexico, it is important to know that no American or Canadian insurance company covers damages or injuries resulting from car accidents, whether the car belongs to you or not.

It is therefore essential to obtain **comprehensive insurance** from a Mexican company. Expect to pay about $230 US for two weeks' coverage.

For those driving in from the northern, eastern or central United States, the city of Laredo, Texas, remains one of the main gateways into Mexican territory. It is best to take out a Mexican car-insurance policy on the American side, in Laredo (Texas), rather than in Mexico, in Nuevo Laredo, in the State of Nuevo Léon (see below). There are, in fact, a few Mexican insurance companies in the American border town. Sanbourn is the preferred insurance firm of Americans, easily recognizable by its sombrero logo.

In Laredo, the Río Grande runs along the Mexican-US border. On either side of the "international bridge" are American and Mexican customs. Nuevo Laredo, in the State of Nuevo Léon, is the first city on the Mexican side.

In Nuevo Laredo, visitors do not require a permit to drive within 24 kilometres (15 miles) of the border. However, at the exit of the "international bridge", drivers must stop at a green or red light indicating whether to proceed or submit to a search. You must then drive to the customs offices, located a little farther (turn right on the first street after crossing the "international bridge"), to obtain the **tourist card** (*tarjeta de turista*) as well as a **temporary import license** for your vehicle. There are no real signs pointing out the way to the customs and immigration office. Thus is it best to ask for a map of Nuevo Laredo while at the insurance company. Above all, be patient — particularly on the eve of a holiday.

You must first go to the immigration (*migración*) counter, where, after your proof of citizenship has been checked, you will be given a form. Once duly filled out and signed, this form constitutes as your tourist card, which you must keep with you at all times for the length of your stay. The second step consists of making photocopies (*fotocopiado*) of the various documents (driver's license, registration or title deed, insurance, etc) related to driving and your vehicle's temporary import. These documents must then be remitted to the *banjercito* counter. If you're driving a rental car, or if the registration is not in your name, you will have to provide a notarized deed drawn up by the car-rental company or the vehicle's owner giving you authorization to travel outside the country in which it was registered. Customs duties of about $12 US must be paid and are payable by credit card; those who wish to pay in cash will have to shell out a lot more. A sticker will then be applied to the inside the vehicle, on the driver's side. This sticker as well as the various documents, must be returned at the same place before leaving Mexican territory. Permits are valid for 180 days.

You will then come upon a last checkpoint 24 kilometres past the border for a final check before taking to the open road.

We cannot stress enough how essential it is to return the permits to the authorities before leaving the country. Unfortunately, the offices are not always at the border crossing; you should thus make inquiries before lining up at the US border.

**PRACTICAL INFORMATION**

### Gasoline

Because there are fewer gas stations in Mexico than in other North American countries, it is advisable always to fill up whenever the gas gauge shows the tank to be half full. Credit cards are not accepted in any gas stations; you must therefore pay in cash.

### Two Important Tips

Make sure the gas-pump meter reads zero before you fill up, and figure out how much change you will be given. Do not tip the pump attendant, but do give a few pesos to the employee who cleans your car windows, provided of course you've first agreed to it.

**Driving and the Highway Code**

As a safety measure, motorists should only drive between 8am and 8pm or until sundown. At night, the domestic or wild animals that cross the road can cause accidents. Also, *bandidos* often commit their misdeeds at night. Moreover, as these same bandits increasingly strike during the day, drivers must be twice as cautious. At the end of the day, it is best to opt for a hotel or "motel-hotel" with a night-security staff. As well, be sure not to leave any of your belongings in the car (suitcases, cameras, money, traveller's cheques and personal documents). If a guard or a parking valet asks you to entrust them with your car key, let the person in question know that your Mexican insurer, and the law of the country, prohibits any Mexican citizen from driving said vehicle without you at their side. In Puerto Vallarta, one story goes that a European woman had lent her car to her Mexican husband-to-be so that he could make a few last-minute purchases for the wedding. Police officers, oblivious to convention, unscrupulously seized the vehicle causing a lot of red tape for the prenuptials.

All drivers should keep photocopies of their (Mexican) car-insurance policy, driver's license, passport and tourist card in their glove compartment. The tourist card is issued to everyone by customs officers upon entering Mexico (see p 47). All original documents should be kept in a safe spot within easy reach, such as your handbag, briefcase, money belt or jacket. If you stop to stretch your legs or for a coffee break along the way, hide anything of value and lock the car doors before getting out of the car.

**Roadside Assistance**

The country's main roads and highways, particularly those in touristed areas, are patrolled by *Angeles Verdes* ("green angels"), green government pick-up trucks driven by mechanics who not only make minor repairs and supply gas and oil at cost price, but provide towing assistance to tourists and locals alike.

**Military Roadblocks**

On major and minor roads, and more rarely on highways, it is not uncommon to encounter a military roadblock. The reasons for these controls are many: "manhunts", drug prevention, vehicle checks, verification of travellers' identification, etc.

**Invaluable Advice**

If you encounter a military or police roadblock and are not signalled to stop, continue on your way while avoiding eye contact with any soldier or police officer on duty: civilians who stare at a government representative arouse suspicion. If you are ordered to stop, do not fail to comply. Refusal to do so will lead the soldiers — all of whom are armed with machine guns — to take drastic measures indeed. And a few metres farther, lookouts will activate a board with beveled pipes across the road to blow all four of your tires in one full swoop. Of concern is the inexperience of these young soldiers whose average age does not exceed twenty. You should therefore only stop if ordered to do so. Should this happen, stay calm and make no sudden movements, or this may make them nervous. Only when the soldiers speak to you should you look them in the eye. Though if they only speak Spanish, it is easy to understand if they simply want to check your papers or search the back trunk and the inside of your car. In the latter case, do not open the trunk automatically! Get out of the car and open the trunk yourself. Remain on the spot throughout the search, because in the past, certain corrupt soldiers have slipped drugs into the car and then threatened its passengers with a jail sentence if they do not pay them the infamous *mordida*, which literally means "your money or your life". Also of considerable note is that, should you forget your priceless driver's license, registration and insurance papers, the vehicle will be impounded right then and there! The vehicle will then be sent by the military authorities to the State capital, obliging some to go retrieve their car several hundred kilometres farther: 535 kilometres from Puerto Vallarta in Guadalajara and 268 kilometres from Puerto Vallarta in Tepic, the capital of the neighbouring State of Nayarit. If such a misfortune occurs, try at least to remove your personal belongings from the car. Moreover, the laborious steps that must be taken to regain possession of an impounded vehicle involve never-ending red tape.

This can take several weeks, even months in certain cases, and necessitates travelling to the capital several times. Finally, when you are at last summoned to retrieve your vehicle, bring a witness or, better yet, the consul from your country. Once there, check the vehicle thoroughly. Why? Because someone else could have slipped drugs into your car, and you will have to relive the whole ordeal! Another tip: notify your country's consulate or embassy immediately and ask them to intercede on your behalf as soon as possible.

## Car Rental Companies

Avis
International Airport
☎1-11-12, 1-16-57 or
01-800-70-77

Budget
Avenida Paseo de las Palmas,
n° 1004
*(north of the city, in the hotel zone)*
☎21-12-10, 22-67-60 or
01-800-7000-17

De Alba
Aquiles Serdán, n° 194
*(2 streets south of Río Cuale)*
☎2-30-66, 2-29-59 or
2-35-76

Dollar
Francisco Medina Ascencio,
n° 1728
*(north of the city, in front of the Sheraton)*
☎3-13-54 or
91 (800) 9-00-10;

International Airport,
☎2-17-27

National
International Airport
☎1-12-26,  2-05-15   or
01-800-69-888

Quick
Francisco Medina Ascencio,
n° 1712
*(north of the city, facing the Sheraton)*
☎2-40-10

Thrifty
Francisco Medina Ascencio,
no. 1712
☎4-07-75

## Distances between Puerto Vallarta
## and other Cities in Mexico

Barra de Navidad: 210 km / 130 mi
Chapala: 390 km / 242 mi
Ciudad Guzmán: 425 km / 264 mi
Colotlán: 541 km / 336 mi
Guadalajara: 535 km / 332 mi
Lagos de Moreno: 340 km / 211 mi
Manzanillo: 285 km / 177 mi
Mazamitla: 473 km / 293 mi
Tapalpa: 470 km / 292 mi
Mexico City: 918 km / 570 mi
Puerto San Blas: 103 km / 64 mi
Tepic: 268 km / 166 mi

PRACTICAL
INFORMATION

## Taxis

Taxi service is available in all tourist areas, as well as in downtown Puerto Vallarta. Taxis are probably the most efficient and safest means of getting around. Over 1,000 cabs operate in the city 24 hours a day. The drivers charge a fixed rate, as there are no meters. Within the downtown area, the fares are around 13 pesos, and transportation between the Marina and downtown costs 25 pesos. The hotels post the fares for the most popular destinations. It is always best to confirm the cost of the trip with the driver before you set out. Furthermore, tipping is not necessary unless you have baggage with you. You can also make arrangements with the driver to take you on sightseeing trips outside of town.

## Buses (*chivas*)

Public buses, known as *camiónes* in Mexico, are numerous and go just about everywhere, offering a novel and economic means of travelling all around Puerto Vallarta. They are dilapidated and uncomfortable, but fast. Often packed, they are not the best option when you are carrying baggage, however. It will cost you about two pesos to ride up to 20 km outside of town and 4 pesos and 5 pesos to go to Nuevo Vallarta and Punta de Mita respectively. There is no real schedule, but you'll never have to wait longer than five minutes, whichever direction you are heading in. The final destination, be it a hotel or a suburb, will be written on the windshield. For example, *Olas* (Olas Altas) is a street in the southern part of town, near the Los Muertos beach; *Boca* (Boca de Tomatlán) is farther south via Mismaloya; *Centro* goes downtown; *Tunel* skirts round the centre of town; *Ptillal* or *Hotels* head north to the hotels; *Marina Vallarta* and *Vidafel* go a bit further north to the marina; and *Aéroporto-Airport*, *Juntas* and *Ixtapas* go to the airport. You can also ask the driver which bus to take to get where you want to go. The stops, indicated by signs, are usually located at intersections. All you have to do is wave and the driver will stop. Buses run every day from 6am to 11:30pm.

All sorts of friendly encounters occur on the bus, and it is not uncommon for the person seated next to you to give in to his or her curiosity by asking you where you're from.

## Coach Service

Different coach companies link Puerto Vallarta with other cities in Mexico. These buses are usually quite comfortable; some even have televisions, and serve coffee and sandwiches.

Elite
Avenida Insurgentes, n° 329
Colonia Emiliano Zapata
☎3-11-17

Estrella Blanca
189 Insurgentes
☎2-06-13 or 2-66-66
or
Medina Brasil no. 1279
☎2-69-43

E.T.N.
Lazaro Cárdenas, n° 258
☎3-29-99 or 3-06-46

Primera Plus
Lazaro Cárdenas, n° 258
☎2-69-86 or 3-11-17

Del Pacifico
Insurgentes, n° 282
☎2-56-22
or
Insurgentes no. 100
☎2-10-15

## Boat-taxis

You'll find motorized boat-taxis at the pier of the Los Muertos beach, in Boca de Tomatlán and at the Marina Vallarta. These can take you just about anywhere in the Bahía de Banderas. The most popular destinations are the Mismaloya, Las Animas, Quimixto and Yelapa beaches. The boats leave the pier at around 11am and return at 4:30pm. It is wise to check the schedules the day before your outing. The return trip will cost you around 120 pesos. Certain agencies offer round-trip packages including breakfast and lunch for 180 to 230 pesos.

## Streetcars

Visitors can take a 20-minute tour of the city aboard a streetcar *(every day 10am to 2pm and 4pm to 8:30pm)*, which sets out from the Plaza de Armas, Puerto Vallarta's main square. This tour is sponsored by a number of downtown businesses, so don't be surprised if various restaurants, clubs, shops and other establishments figure on the itinerary. The service is free, but a tip of two or three pesos is appreciated.

PRACTICAL
INFORMATION

## Scooters

Scooters can be rented by the hour or by the day in Puerto Vallarta. Make sure that the rental charge includes insurance. You won't see many motorcyclists here, for a very good reason: the secondary roads leading south are unpaved and full of twists and turns; the traffic doesn't flow well and the motorists are not at all disciplined. Don't forget, furthermore, that the streets of Puerto Vallarta are paved with cobblestone, which doesn't make things any easier when you're on a scooter.

**Scooter Rentals**

Moto Rent
Francisco Medina Ascencio no. 39
☎2-17-65

Motos Vejar
Perú no. 1204
☎2-31-39

---

## Hitchhiking

---

Risky business! It is highly inadvisable to hitchhike in Mexico.

---
MONEY AND BANKING
---

---

## Currency

---

The country's currency is the nuevo peso or peso. There are 10, 20, 50, 100, 200 and 500 peso bills and 1, 5, 10, 20 and 50 peso coins, as well as 5, 10, 20 and 50 centavo pieces. Prices are often also listed in US dollars, especially in touristy areas. Be careful: there are still a few old pesos in circulation, and they are only worth 1% of the new peso. In a place like a dimly lit bar, someone might try to swindle you by slipping you your change in old pesos.

All prices quoted in this guide are in US dollars.

Mexican currency is subject to major fluctuations, and has been devalued numerous times in recent years. The exchange rates for various foreign currencies are listed below. These were in effect at press time, and are only intended to give you a general idea.

---

## Banks

---

The local banks are open from 9am to 3pm, Monday to Friday. Most of them will change Canadian and US dollars; fewer will change other foreign currencies. It is generally to your advantage to travel in Mexico with US dollars, as the exchange rates are better. A number of banks have automated teller machines that accept debit and credit cards.

Banamex (Visa, Mastercard)
180 Zaragoza
*(on the plaza, opposite the Vierge de Guadalupe church)*
☎2-08-30, 2-19-98, 2-06-93 or 01-800-706-66

American Express
660 Morelos
☎3-29-55, 3-29-91, 3-29-29 or 01-800-00-33-33

Mastercard, Visa
277 Hidalgo, office 3
☎316-58-59

## Exchange Offices

Various exchange offices are located throughout Puerto Vallarta near the hotels and in the centre of town. Rates vary little from one place to the next. American and Canadian dollars, either in cash or travellers', cheques are the easiest to exchange. When changing the latter you will generally be required to show identification with a photo and signature or a passport. Exchange offices that deal in other currencies are located near the *malecón*.

Euromex
Zaragoza, no 176
*(downtown on the Plaza de Armas)*
9am to 1pm

Casa Tequila
Paseo Díaz Ordaz
*(at the bend in the malecón)*
9am to 9pm

Centenario
Morelos, n° 480
9am to 9pm

## Exchange Rates

| | |
|---|---|
| $1 US    = 9.35 NP | 1 NP = $0.11 US |
| $1 CAN  = 6.36 NP | 1 NP = $0.16 CAN |
| 1 £      = 14.49 NP | 1 NP = 0.07 £ |
| $1 Aust = 6.23 NP | 1 NP = $0.16 Aust |
| $1 NZ   = 4.94 NP | 1 NP = $0.20 NZ |
| 1000 LIT = 4.92 NP | 1 NP = 202 LIT |
| 100 PTA = 5.73 NP | 1 NP = 17.40 PTA |
| 10 BF   = 2.36 NP | 1 NP = 4.22 BF |
| 1 SF    = 5.93 NP | 1 NP = 0.17 SF |
| 1 fl    = 4.33 NP | 1 NP = 0.23 fl |
| 1 DM    = 4.87 NP | 1 NP = 0.20 DM |

## Exchanging Money

It is illegal and inadvisable to exchange money in the street. Given the risks (theft, counterfeit bills, etc.) and the small amount of money you stand to save, it is far better to change your money at a bank or an exchange office. For the best rate of exchange, make a cash withdrawal on your credit card; this will save you about 2%, which is generally more than the interest you'll have to pay when you get back. For the same reason, it is best to pay for purchases with your credit card whenever possible.

## Travellers' Cheques

It is always wise to keep most of your money in travellers' cheques, which, when in US dollars, are sometimes accepted in restaurants, hotels and shops. They are also easy to exchange in most banks and foreign exchange offices. Be sure to keep a copy of the serial numbers of the cheques in a separate place, so if ever they are lost, the company that issued them can replace them quickly and easily. Nevertheless, always keep some cash on hand.

## Credit Cards

Credit cards, especially Visa and MasterCard, are accepted in a large number of businesses. In addition to being easy to use, they offer the best exchange rates, and it is therefore better to pay for as many of your purchases with them. When using a credit card, you will need to present your passport and write its number on the bill.

Banamex (Visa, MC)
Zaragoza, n° 180
*(on the square, facing the Guadalupe church)*
9am to 3pm
☎2-08-30, 2-19-98 ou 2-06-93

American Express
Villa Vallarta
Suite H-6
☎3-29-55 or 3-29-95

MasterCard
Hidalgo, n° 277
Suite 3
☎2-32-03, 2-39-02 or 2-06-42

Visa
☎95(800)847-2911

## SHOPPING

The local shops are usually open from 9am to 8pm or 9pm, Monday to Saturday. However, in certain areas, such as the *malecón* and the Marina, the stores are open on Sunday and often close later than elsewhere. The prices there are considerably higher than on streets like Insurgentes and Lazaro Cárdenas, located in the southern part of town, where you'll find shoe and clothing stores, and even a place that sells painted ceramic tiles. In fact, the farther you go from the touristy areas, the lower the prices are. Many native artisans, from the Huichol community for one, have set up co-ops. Local vendors, a number of whom are natives as well, buy their stock from these co-ops or directly from the artisans. They then sell the crafts in the major tourist spots and resort areas — sometimes on the beaches in Puerto Vallarta and right outside town.

Puerto Vallarta is home to a number of shops run by artisans' cooperatives. These retail outlets offer visitors the best possible prices, as well as a good choice of magnificent handicrafts. Silver- and gold-plated objects, dishes, muticoloured pottery, paintings, jewellery, fanciful wooden masks, fabrics, blown glass and basketry are some of the loveliest purchases you can make here. Near the Museo del Cuale, in the centre of Isla Cuale, you'll also find a string of craft stalls, most of which are open from 10am to 4pm and from 4pm to 9pm. This crafts market is better known as "El Mercado del Río Cuale".

**Bargaining:** Although bargaining might seem to be a standard practice in some shops, it can also be considered impolite. Often the prices are fair to begin with and, especially when it comes to handicrafts, bargaining can be inappropriate. The vendors on the beaches are used to being bargained with, but even that requires a certain amount of tact.

## MAIL AND TELECOMMUNICATIONS

### Mail

It costs 2.50 pesos to send a postcard or letter to Europe, 2.10 pesos to countries in North, South and Central America.

**Post Office**

Mexpost
Juarez, n° 584
Mon to Fri 9am to 6pm, Sat 9am to 1pm

### Telephone

The **area code** for Puerto Vallarta is **322**.

## Calling Mexico from Abroad

From Canada: Dial 011-52 + 322 (for Puerto Vallarta) + local number.

From the United States: Dial 011-52 + 322 (for Puerto Vallarta) + local number.

From Great Britain: Dial 00-52 + 322 (for Puerto Vallarta) + local number.

## Calling Abroad from Mexico

As a general rule, it is more economical to call collect; this is the best option for Canadian, American and British citizens wishing to call someone in their native country.

To call Canada: **Canada Direct**: 00-800-010-1990 + area code + local number, or wait for an operator to help you.

To call the United States: **AT&T**: 00-800-462-4240 + area code + local number, or wait for an operator to help you.
**Sprint**: 00-800-877-8000 + area code + local number, or wait for an operator to help you.
**MCI**: 00-800-674-7000 + area code + local number, or wait for an operator to help you.

To call Great Britain: **BT**: *791 + area code + local number, or wait for an operator to help you.

**For long-distance calls within Mexico, dial 0 + local number.**

Operator assistance:

- for international calls, dial 090
- for calls within Mexico, dial 020
- for information, dial 040

There are public telephones all over town. To use these, you must have a phone card, which may be purchased in pharmacies for 50 pesos. There are also a number of telephones owned by a private American company, which accept Visa, MasterCard and American Express; take note, however, that you will be charged an exorbitant rate in US dollars if you use one of these.

---

## FESTIVALS AND HOLIDAYS

In Mexico, several Christian holy days are official holidays. In addition to these, there are a number of other public holidays commemorating the great deeds of the country's historical figures. Mexicans love a good *fiesta*. This passion is translated into scores of official and regional celebrations — no fewer than 6,000 annually, not including more "spontaneous" events like weddings, christenings and birthdays, even funerals.

---

### Calendar of Events

---

Here is a list of the major Mexican holidays, organized by month:

**January**

1 - **New Year's Day**: The "Año Nuevo" is ushered in with major festivities. In the cities, Mexicans mark the occasion with all sorts of mass gatherings, and agricultural fairs are held all over the country.

6 - **Twelfth Night**: Mexican children receive their New Year's gifts on this, the "Día de Reyes" or Day of Kings. Traditionally, a Twelfth Night cake with a tiny doll hidden in it is served at mealtime. The person who is served the piece containing the doll must invite all those present at the table to dinner on February 2, Candlemas.

17 - **San Antonio Abad's Day**: In rural Mexico, even animals have holidays. On San Antonio Abad's Day, all domesticated animals, be they house pets or farm animals, are groomed and arrayed in lavishly decorated garb, then led into the local churches, where they are blessed during a religious ceremony.

## February

2 - **Candlemas**: On February 2, celebrations are held in all the streets of all the cities, towns and villages in Mexico, and the main arteries are lit up with multicoloured lanterns. The occasion is marked by parades — sometimes quite extravagant ones — as well as bullfights either in the Spanish tradition or, often, with *rejoneadores* (toreadors on horseback).

5 - **Constitution Day**: As indicated by its name, this day, "Día de la Constitución", commemorates the constitutions of 1857 and 1917, which still apply to all Mexican political institutions.

**Mardi Gras**: The pre-Lenten festivities are held in February or March, depending on the year. Each town has its own carnival. In Puerto Vallarta, as in many other resort areas, people get decked out in costumes, parade through town to music performed by the best local bands, and dance on the public squares and in the streets.

24 - **Flag Day**: Mexicans are proud of their glorious heritage, and have a great deal of respect for their tricoloured (green, white and red) flag, which has an eagle, symbol of prosperity on its white stripe (see inset, "The Eagle, Symbol of Mexico", p 14). Throughout the country, February 24 is a day of pride and an affirmation of national identity.

## March

13 - **Annual witches' conference**: Mexican witches (*brujas*) hold an annual get-together at Catemaco Lake, attracting large numbers of followers.

18 - **Anniversary of the expropriation of foreign oil companies**: In Mexico, everything associated with autonomy and sovereignty is viewed with the utmost respect.

21 - **President Benito Juárez García's birthday**: Mexico's most revered politician, Benito Juárez García, was of indigenous descent. He became president of the country's first liberal government, which, as of 1855, undertook a series of constitutional reforms. March 21 is enthusiastically celebrated through-

out the country, especially in his birthplace, the state of Oaxaca, of which he was governor.

**Holy Week** (in March or April, depending on the year): The "Semana Santa" is the most important religious celebration in Mexico. It starts on Palm Sunday and is marked by festivities all over the country. Some of these celebrations are positively gigantic. Among the most impressive are the Ixtapalapa Passion Play in Mexico City, the silent processions in San Luís Potosi and San Miguel de Allende, and the candle-lit procession in Taxco. Equally spectacular religious processions in many other towns attract thousands of believers. Not to be outdone, the seaside city of Puerto Vallarta is overrun by thousands of visitors from Guadalajara, the capital of the state of Jalisco, and even from the national capital, Mexico City, during this period.

### April

**Easter** (date varies depending on the year): Mexicans use Easter vacation as an opportunity to escape city life and enjoy a trip to the sea or to the countryside, or visit their family.

### May

1 - **Labour Day**: Working people all over Mexico celebrate this public holiday with parades promoting national and international solidarity among workers.

3 - **Holy Cross Day**: On this day, construction workers hoist huge crosses onto all unfinished buildings, thus honouring the sacred symbol of the Christian faith. Holy Cross Day is also celebrated with family picnics and fireworks.

5 - **Cinco de Mayo**: The Cinco de Mayo commemorates the Mexican victory over the French army in 1862, during the famous Battle of Puebla, when 4,000 men armed with outdated weapons managed to drive back 6,000 elite soldiers sent by Emperor Napoleon III.

**Mother's Day** (a Sunday in May; date varies from year to year): As in many countries, the "Día de las Madres" is a family celebration. It is a special day for all mothers, who receive gifts and flowers for the occasion.

15 - **San Isidro's Day:** San Isidro is the patron saint of farmers and livestock. He is the one people pray to to make it rain enough for the crops to flourish.

## June

24 - **Midsummer's Day** (feast of St. John the Baptist): Mexicans hold fairs, religious gatherings and aquatic competitions.

## August

2 - **Cuauhtémoc's Day:** The most grandiose of all Mexican celebrations, in memory of Cuauhtémoc, the last Aztec emperor (he was hanged by Cortés in 1524), takes place on the square named after him in Mexico City, where dances and official ceremonies are held.

## September

15 and 16: **Independence Day:** The festivities last two days, both official holidays. There is not a single place in Mexico that doesn't celebrate the 1810 Declaration of Independence with great pomp. The Mexican people could never forget this historic declaration, which, after Father Hidalgo's call for a mass uprising, made Mexico a sovereign state, free at last from all foreign rule. At the stroke of 11pm, there is a re-enactment of "El Grito", Hidalgo's famous appeal to his compatriots, on all the public squares in all the towns and cities in the country. In the federal capital, Mexico City, on Constitution Square, the Mexican President opens the traditional ceremonies by addressing the diplomatic corps and the nation as a whole. The entire country celebrates with festivities and fireworks.

## October

1 to 31 - **The Guadalajara October Festivals:** One of Mexico's largest cultural and sporting events is held in Guadalajara, the

capital of the state of Jalisco and the second biggest city in the country. Throughout the month of October, the city is the scene of all sorts of activities, including plays, films, musicals, athletic competitions, etc.

12 - **"Raza" Day**: Reluctant to commemorate that controversial event, Columbus's "discovery" of America, Mexicans concentrate instead on the blending of the great Amerindian civilizations of the past with European civilization.

15 to 31 - **The Guanajuato Cervantés Festival**: A festival honouring celebrated Spanish author Miguel de Cervantés is held each year in Guanajuato. It is entirely devoted to the arts: theatre events, troubadours, singing and poetry recitals, classical music, etc.

**November**

1 - **The President's State of the Nation Address**: Every year on this public holiday the Mexican President addresses Congress, and the speech is broadcasted all over the country.

1 and 2 - **All Saints' Day**: The most mysterious of all Mexican *fiestas* is definitely the "Día de los Muertos". This blend of Amerindian and Christian traditions is another excellent example of the unique character of the Mexican people. On All Saints' Day, the nation's confectioners go all out; in keeping with tradition, all sorts of sweets shaped like skulls, skeletons and coffins are displayed on counters at grocery stores, pastry shops and all sorts of other businesses for customers eager to stock up on goodies. Large numbers of people march in procession through the cemeteries, which are decorated and lit up (at night) for the occasion. It is also on these two days that families put flowers on the graves of close relatives who have died, thus keeping their memory alive.

20 - **Anniversary of the Mexican Revolution**: Millions of Mexicans lost their lives during the Revolution, which lasted from 1910 to 1920. On November 20, the country commemorates the beginning of this civil war.

10th to 20th — **Fiesta del Mar** kicks off the tourist season in Puerto Vallarta. The festival features several activities, including the México Boat Show, a fishing tournament and regattas. Among the other events on the program are the food festival, in which numerous restaurants participate, each establishment offering a menu prepared by a foreign chef invited for the occasion.

## December

**1 to 11 - Festival of the Virgin of Guadalupe:** For two weeks, the whole city gets ready to celebrate. Decorations are put up everywhere, and all sorts of performances take place on the public squares: *mariachis, trio guitarra*, bands, *rendallas* (guitar, violin, mandolin, accordion, etc.), folk dancing, Hispanic and native dances, plays, etc. On the last two days, a number of streets are closed off (you'll have to walk to get downtown), and it's time for the parades, which all the local businesses participate in. People walk into town from the surrounding villages; colourful allegorical floats, including one dedicated to the Virgin, make their way to the cathedral, where the crowd sings the *Mañanit*, a song of thanks to the Virgin *(schedule of daily events available at the Dirección Regional de Turismo de Puerto Vallarta: Juárez e Independencia, Planta Baja Palacio Municipal, ☎322-2-02-42, 3-07-44 or 3-08-44, ≈322-2-02-43).*

PRACTICAL INFORMATION

**12 - Feast day of the Virgin of Guadalupe:** This is Mexico's most important religious holiday. Tens of thousands of pilgrims make their way to the cathedral in Mexico City to see the famous robe miraculously imprinted with the image of the Virgin, who, according to popular belief, gave the garment to an Aztec peasant named Juan Diego when she appeared to him in December 1531.

**16 - 24: Las "Posadas":** On the days leading up to Christmas, Mexicans commemorate Joseph and Mary's trip to Bethlehem with numerous processions and parades. This is a great time of the year for kids, who get to break open *piñatas* and feast on the candies inside. Music, singing and dancing are all on the agenda.

**25 - Christmas:** Mexicans generally spend Christmas Day with their family.

# MISCELLANEOUS

## Electricity

Local electricity operates at 110 volts AC, as in North America. Plugs must have flat pins, so Europeans will need both a converter and a wall socket adapter.

## Women Travellers

Women travelling alone in this city should not have any problems. In general, locals are friendly and not too aggressive. Although men treat women with respect and harassment is relatively rare, Mexicans will undoubtedly flirt with female travellers—politely, though. Of course, a minimum amount of caution is required; for example, women should avoid walking alone through poorly lit areas at night. Furthermore, wearing clothes that are not too revealing will probably spare you some aggravation in this primarily Catholic country.

## Time Zones

Puerto Vallarta is one hour behind Eastern Standard Time, six hours behind Greenwich Mean Time and seven hours behind continental Europe.

## Prices, Taxes and Tips

The local **tax** is called the **IVA**. For ordinary purchases, it is almost always included in the price shown. The term *Propina incluida* means that the tip is included. When it is not included, add between 10% and 15% to the bill.

## Weights and Measures

Mexico uses the metric system. Here are some useful conversions:

**Weights**
1 pound (lb) = 454 grams (g)
1 kilogram (kg) = 2.2 pounds (lbs)

**Linear Measure**
1 inch = 2.54 centimetres (cm)
1 foot (ft) = 30 centimetres (cm)
1 mile = 1.6 kilometres (km)
1 kilometre (km) = 0.63 miles
1 metre (m) = 39.37 inches

**Land Measure**
1 acre = 0.4047 hectares
1 hectare = 2.471 acres

**Volume Measure**
1 U.S. gallon (gal) = 3.79 litres
1 U.S. gallon (gal) = 0.83 imperial gallons

**Temperature**
To convert °F into °C: subtract 32, divide by 9, multiply by 5
To convert °C into °F: multiply by 9, divide by 5, add 32.

PRACTICAL
INFORMATION

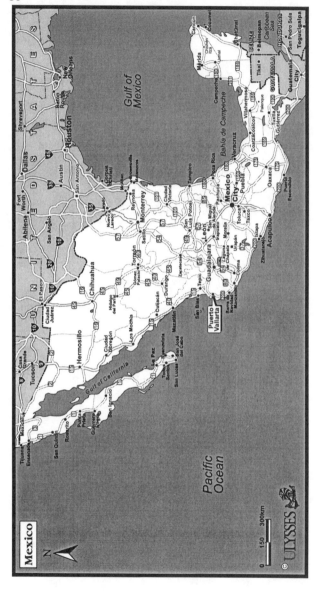

## SIGHTS AND BEACHES

**V**isitors will find that Puerto Vallarta and its beaches make for a richly rewarding vacation. The best way to experience this wonderful seaside resort on the Pacific is to tap into the rhythm of its daily life, as the Mexicans do, by strolling the Malecón, nosing around inside one of the city's magnificent art galleries, visiting a museum or simply loafing on one of its many beaches.

  THE OLD TOWN ★★

### Isla Cuale and the Northern Río Cuale

The Río Cuale (Cuale River) divides the city of Puerto Vallarta in two. An islet of the same name (Isla Cuale) sits in the middle of the river. Two bridges link Puerto Vallarta's two sections. Each bridge is one-way; the one to the north leads to the Old Town and the other to the southern district.

The northern district, downtown Puerto Vallarta's historic city centre, is definitely the more interesting area. Its attractions include the Malecón, the seaside promenade overlooking the

## Guided Tours

A coach tour *($11 US)* is a good way to see Puerto Vallarta's major attractions: the Templo de Guadalupe, the Malecón and "Gringo Gulch", in the upper part of town, behind the cathedral, where Americans built magnificent houses, including the one where Richard Burton and Elizabeth Taylor lived (Casa Kimberley). The tour continues south of the city, into the Conchas Chinas residential area, a wealthy hillside neighbourhood. Visits to Marina Vallarta and the main shopping centres are included as well. Other tours include hikes in the Sierra Madre rain forest or visits to plantations *($15 US)*. You can also take an organized day-trip to San Blas *($45 US)*, a small fishing village to the north, in the state of Nayarit, or fly to Guadalajara for a day or a night *($65 to $75 US, plus airport charges)*.

breathtaking Bahía de La Banderas (Bay of Flags). The area's vibrant streets and public squares offer a great opportunity to feel the pulse of everyday life in Puerto Vallarta. And the architecture of the old buildings, topped with ochre orange-coloured tiles, is absolutely lovely.

The section to the south of the Río Cuale is home to the city's biggest concentration of hotels and restaurants. The bus stations and the Playa Los Muertos are also found in this area.

### Church of the Virgin of Guadalupe ★ Templo de Guadalupe

Though it dates from the turn of the century, this church *(Calle Hidalgo, near the Plaza de Armas)* is a fine example of the architectural style that arrived with the Spanish and the advent of Catholicism. It is dedicated to Mexico's patron saint, the Virgin of Guadalupe, whose feast day is December 12. She was a dark-skinned virgin who appeared in a vision to the Indian Juan Diego on the hill where the Aztecs worshipped Tonantzin, the mother of their gods; she thus symbolizes the blending of the two religions. The church is capped with a crown that looks to some observers like the crown that belonged to the Empress Carlotta, wife of the notorious Emperor Maximilian, who

**Puerto Vallarta**

**ACCOMMODATIONS**

1. Buenaventura
2. Continental Plaza
3. El Pescador
4. Fiesta Americana
5. Holiday Inn
6. Kristal Vallarta
7. Los Tules
8. Qualton Club & Spa Vallarta
9. Sheraton Buganvillias
10. Suites Coral

**RESTAURANTS**

1. Avanzaré
2. El Chiringuito
3. El Mirador
4. La Bamba
5. La Guacamaya
6. La Hacienda
7. La Villita
8. Las Gaviotas
9. Rio Grande
10. Tangaroa

Bahía de Banderas

See map of downtown

© ULYSSES

SIGHTS AND BEACHES

## Strolling Along El Malecón ★★★
### (Seaside Promenade)

Those strolling along El Malecón, a long seaside promenade, will come upon several contemporary sculptures, including the most famous, a bronze by Rafael Zamaripa representing a naked child riding a *caballito de mar* (sea horse), which measures close to 3 metres. *La Fuente de los Delfines* (The Fountain of Dolphins), by artist Octavio Gonzales symbolizes Puerto Vallarta and its twin city, Santa Barbara, California. Among the other works gracing the promenade are *Nostalgia*, by Ramiz Barquet, the creator of the magnificent *El Pescador* (The Fisherman), located near the Mercado Municipal; the *Neptune and Nereid* sculpture, as well as the works of Alenjandro Colunga and Adrián Reynoso, *La Naturaleza Como Madre*, a stylized imitation of an ocean wave, not to mention the surrealist high-backed benches. The promenade also boasts an open-air amphitheatre, situated near the famous Los Arcos ("The Arches"), where all sorts of activities and cultural events take place. The Malecón, where the blazing sunset is at its most dazzling, comes to life at sundown.

On the other side of the Malecón, a naive-style fresco by Manuel Lepe depicting the history of Puerto Vallarta adorns the steps of the Palacio Municipal. The Paseo Díaz Ordaz is lined with souvenir shops and more upscale boutiques, as well as scores of cafés, bars, snack bars and restaurants.

ruled Mexico during the 1860s. The crown, virtually the city's coat of arms, has recently been repaired after being damaged in the last earthquake. Stop in during your wanderings to soak up the atmosphere in this peaceful place, which is pleasantly cool as well as educational.

### Museo del Cuale ★ (Museum of Anthropology and Archeology)

Inhabited for nearly 20 centuries, the entire Bahía de Banderas is rich in archaeological treasures. Major digs are carried out in the State of Jalisco to preserve the many traces of the region's past; after all, the area was home to up to 100,000 people

**Puerto Vallarta** | **Downtown**

### ● ATTRACTIONS

1. Templo de Guadalupe
2. El Malecón
3. Museo del Cuale

### ○ ACCOMMODATIONS

1. Brisas del Mar
2. Casa Kimberley
3. Encino
4. Gloria del Mar - Maxim's Suites
5. Hotel Alegre
6. Hotel Suites Emperador
7. Los Arcos Suites
8. Los Arcos Vallarta-Hotel
9. Meza del Mar
10. Molino de Agua
11. Paco Paco - Descanso del Sol
12. Playa Los Arcos
13. Plaza Corazón
14. Posada de Roger
15. Posada Río Cuale
16. Puerto Vallarta Beach
17. Rosita
18. San Marino Plaza
19. Suites Vista al Oceano
20. Tropicana
21. Vallarta Cora
22. Vallarta Shores
23. Yasmin

### ◇ RESTAURANTS

1. Abadía Bassó
2. Alejandro's
3. Andale
4. Archie's Wok
5. Balam
6. Café Adobe
7. Café de Olla
8. Café des Artistes
9. Café Frankfurt
10. Café Lido
11. Café Maximilien
12. Café Olé
13. Café Trio
14. Chef Roger
15. Coco Tropical
16. Cuiza
17. Daiquiri Dick's
18. El Palomar de los Gonzáles
19. Jalapeño's
20. Karpathos Taverna
21. La Casa de Los Hot Cakes - The Pancake House
22. La Chata
23. La Corbeteña
24. La Dolce Vita
25. La Palapa
26. Le Bistro
27. Los Laureles
28. Los Pibes
29. Nanahuatzin
30. Pipi's
31. Planet Hollywood
32. Ritos Baci
33. Sr. Chico's
34. The Reporter Restaurant

N

Jesús Langarica
Pigila
Guadalupe Sánchez
J.-Ortiz-de-Dominguez
Díaz Ordaz
Moreno
Abasolo
Aldama
Corona
Galeana
Paseo
Mina
Malecón
Iturbide
Juárez
Hidalgo
Zaragoza
Matamoros
Guerrero
Av. Rodríguez
Encino

Bahía de Banderas

Isla Cuale

Aquiles Serdán

F.I. Madero

Playa Olas Altas
Olas Altas
Pino Suárez
Lázaro Cárdenas
Insurgentes
Aguacate
Jacarandaz
Venustiano Carranza
Basilio Badillo
Ignacio Vallarta
Constitución
Manuel M. Diéguez
F. Rodríguez
Rodolfo Gómez
Púlpito
Playa de los Muertos
Amapas
Pilitas
Mismaloya

0    100    200m
Approximate Scale

© ULYSSES

SIGHTS AND BEACHES

before the Spanish arrived. Funeral vases, ceramic busts, domestic objects, jewellery and arms, including arrowheads, have been recovered. The Museo del Cuale (the sign on the building is trilingual — in Spanish, French and English), on the island in the middle of the Río Cuale, offers a collection of artifacts that, while modest, is worth seeing. This museum, along with the larger Guadalajara and Tepic museums, is operated by the National Institute of Anthropology and History.

### Isla Cuale ★

This luxuriant island in the Río Cuale is home to stores, handicraft stalls, restaurants, an art gallery and a cultural centre, in addition to the Museo del Cuale. A park at one end of the island has several benches set among its large trees and flowery groves. Go out to the end of the point for a good view of the river and mountains.

## South of Río Cuale

**Los Muertos ★★** or **Playa del Sol**, its official name, is Puerto Vallarta's most popular beach. It boasts an outstanding location on the majestic Bahía de Banderas (Bay of Flags). The easiest access to this lively spot is from Calle Rodriguez. Numerous hotels and restaurants line the beach, offering lounge chairs under *palapas* (straw umbrellas) for the price of a meal or snack. All day long, sun-worshippers are solicited by strolling vendors, who will usually leave you alone if you aren't interested; if you are, however, there are good buys to be found on this beach: pottery, ceramics, hand-painted mobiles, basketwork, fabric and lots of other attractive handicrafts. A word of caution, though; avoid the skewers of fruits, fish or seafood the vendors offer at mealtime.

To the north of Playa de Los Muertos, just south of the Río Cuale, which divides the city, lies another attractive beach, the **Playa Olas Altas ★**, which means "high waves." The waters off this beach are frequently agitated by the Río Cuale's muddy currents, especially after heavy rains.

**Bahía de Banderas**

© ULYSSES

SIGHTS AND BEACHES

## ○ ACCOMMODATIONS

1. Blue Bay Club Puerto Vallarta
2. Camino Real
3. Hotel Lagunita de Yelapa
4. La Jolla de Mismaloya
5. Majahuitas Resort
6. Presidente InterContinental
7. Vista Bahía

## ◇ RESTAURANTS

1. Acuario and El Anclote
2. Che Che
3. Chico's Paraíso
4. Chino's Paraíso
5. Don Pedro's
6. El Asadero
7. El Embarcadero
8. El Nogalito
9. El Patio Steak House
10. El Set
11. La Iguana Italiana
12. La Noche de la Iguana
13. La Perla
14. Le Kliff
15. Miramar
16. Ramada Miramar

SOUTHERN PUERTO VALLARTA

More superb beaches, smaller but much less crowded, lie to the south of Puerto Vallarta. Secluded along the rocky coastline, **Las Amapas ★** and **Conchas Chinas ★** offer crystal-clear water. A path that begins south of Los Muertos beach leads to these beaches, which sit below a residential neighbourhood whose opulent, boldly designed houses and condominiums seem to hang suspended from the side of the hill. You can also get to these beaches on the bus that runs regularly between Mismaloya and Boca de Tomatlán; ask the driver to let you off at the El Set hotel and restaurant.

It costs just a few pesos to take the bus farther along the coastal road, scenic Highway 200. The shore is dotted with bays and coves rimmed by the lush slopes of the Sierra Madre hills. At the Camino Real hotel, **Las Estacas ★** beach offers some 600 metres of powdery sand. The smaller **Punta Negra ★** and **Macumba ★** beaches are bordered with coconut trees. The sea off these beaches is calm and the water very clean.

Next on the route are the islets of **Los Arcos ★★**, rocky formations sculpted by erosion that rise to a height of 25 metres, dubbed the **Underwater National Park**, followed by **Mismaloya ★★**, where the beach sits along a bay at the mouth of the Mismaloya stream. This area, with its village atmosphere and residents who have carefully preserved many of the old customs and traditions, is very popular among Mexican urbanites. A variety of restaurants and snack bars are clustered on the south shore of the stream (the Ramada Miramar, in the middle is the best). Keep strolling and you'll soon come to a trail at the edge of the water that leads to the site — or at least what's left of it — where *Night of the Iguana* was filmed. You can also rent a boat to go deep-sea fishing or scuba diving around the Los Arcos islands. Tables and chaises longues are available at the Jolla de Mismaloya hotel.

Farther along the road, the bus stops above **Boca de Tomatlán ★**. Walk down the steep road into the centre of this village overlooking the sea. En route, you'll pass a small fruit and vegetable market as well as a little place that makes tortillas, which you take-out or eat warm on the spot. The attractive gold-hued beach runs alongside the Río Tomatlán, which empties into the ocean here. The handful of restaurants along the beach specialize in fish and seafood. The terrain at the water's edge is rocky and the water off the beach is often turbulent because of the river flow, especially during the rainy season (June to September). Water-taxis can take you from here to Las Ánimas, Quimixto and Yelapa beaches.

The road continues along the Tomatlán River, rising into the Sierra Madre's lofty mountains. This panoramic drive to Barra de Navidad is worth the detour, at least as far as Chico's Paraíso restaurant, balanced on the rocks in the Río Los Orcones. There are several waterfalls along the way and at some places young daredevils willingly dive into deep pools to retrieve a few pesos. A taxi travels the road from Boca de Tomatlán; it costs about 25 pesos *($3.50 US)*.

##    THE NORTHERN HOTEL ZONE

Hotels abound in this northern section of Puerto Vallarta. The hotels stand along the **Las Glorias ★★** and **Los Tules ★★** beaches, all the way to Terminal Maritima. Each hotel's beach is marked off with low stone walls and is strictly reserved for guests of that establishment. However, non-guests can enjoy these beaches and their amenities by dining at one of the innumerable restaurants and bars. The ocean is fairly calm in these parts and you may want to try water-skiing or parasailing. long.

After crossing the rushing Río Ameca, which runs along the border between the states of Jalisco and Nayarit, you'll reach an imposing boulevard lined with coconut trees. This road leads to Nuevo Vallarta, a vast compound of deluxe hotels that exudes a Florida-style allure. However, it's not all that easy to make use of Nuevo Vallarta's beaches, because of the location and because its hotels are generally off-limits to non-guests – some are virtual guarded fortresses. Surprisingly, a number of the roads leading to Nuevo Vallarta are very poorly maintained. Many hotels in Nuevo Vallarta offer all-inclusive packages.

The climate gets drier and drier and the vegetation sparser and sparser the closer you get to Punta de Mita, in the southern part of the peninsula, which juts into the Bahía de Banderas. **Manzanilla** ★★ is the first beach you come across, after the village of Cruz de Huanacaxtle. The Miramar restaurant, one of the best places around for the freshest fish and seafood is located here. The beach is subdivided by a stone jetty. The ocean is calm, and its smooth shallow bottom lets swimmers get a good long way from shore. This beach is favoured by Mexican vacationers who strike up conversations with foreign visitors at the drop of a hat.

Five kilometres farther, **Destiladeras** ★★★ is one of the most beautiful beaches in the area. Its waves, sometimes regular and sometimes powerful, are perfect for surfing. A small restaurant on the beach, a fast-food place really, offers *quesadillas* and tacos for the hungry and fruit juice and beer for the thirsty – a good thing, since it's sweltering here.

**Paraíso Escondido** ★★★ (hidden paradise) is the least crowded beach in this region, and difficult to find unless you're a surfer and already familiar with it. A signpost marks the entrance, about 5 km from Destiladeras; from there, you have to follow a trail to the beach. Finally, **El Anclote** ★★, the village at the far end of the bay, also has an excellent beach that's lined with myriad seafood restaurants. Despite big waves, swimming is safe here and you can walk quite far out into the ocean.

  MARINA VALLARTA ★★

This is one of Mexico's prettiest pleasure-craft ports and very popular among sailing enthusiasts. In addition to vacationers who stay in the surrounding hotels and condominiums, the marina attracts many locals looking to partake of everything this immense complex has to offer: a white-sand beach dotted with piers, a wide variety of water sports, flamenco shows and lots of atmosphere. Its 18-hole golf course, sprinkled with lakes, lagoons and luxuriant greenery, is a big draw for golf fanatics. Luxury hotels have recently been built along **Playa El Salado** ★★.

Every two years (in February of odd-numbered years), Marina Vallarta is the setting for the **Marina del Rey-Puerto Vallarta Regatta**. The races start near San Diego, Calif., and end here.

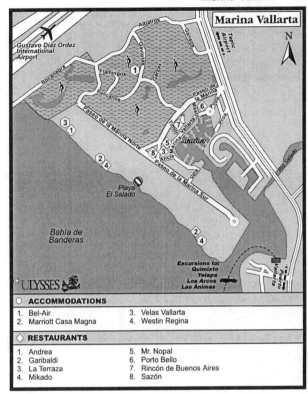

**Marina Vallarta**

○ **ACCOMMODATIONS**

| 1. Bel-Air | 3. Velas Vallarta |
| 2. Marriott Casa Magna | 4. Westin Regina |

◇ **RESTAURANTS**

| 1. Andrea | 5. Mr. Nopal |
| 2. Garibaldi | 6. Porto Bello |
| 3. La Terraza | 7. Rincón de Buenos Aires |
| 4. Mikado | 8. Sazón |

SIGHTS AND BEACHES

During the regatta, a host of activities and festivals are staged at the marina. You can pick up information on the Marina de Vallarta in most hotels and restaurants throughout Puerto Vallarta.

NUEVO VALLARTA

New Vallarta, or "Nuevo Vallarta" in Spanish, is north of the airport, in the State of Narayit, while the "old town" of Puerto Vallarta is in the State of Jalisco. Nuevo Vallarta is more of a tourist complex than an urban area; still, tourists will find most necessary services here as well as good restaurants, bars and

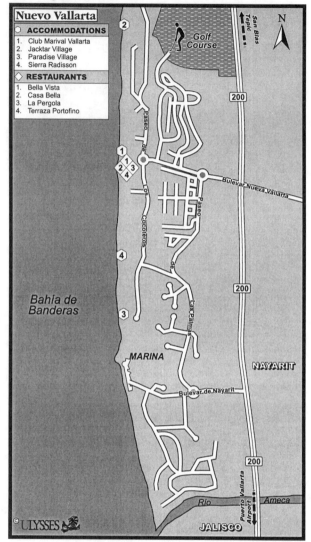

Nuevo Vallarta

○ **ACCOMMODATIONS**
1. Club Marival Vallarta
2. Jacktar Village
3. Paradise Village
4. Sierra Radisson

◇ **RESTAURANTS**
1. Bella Vista
2. Casa Bella
3. La Pergola
4. Terraza Portofino

Golf Course

San Blas Tepic

200

Bulevar Nueva Vallarta

Paseo de Los Cocoteros

200

Bahía de Banderas

Las Palmas

MARINA

NAYARIT

Bulevar de Nayarit

200

Río Ameca

Puerto Vallarta Airport

JALISCO

© ULYSSES

nightclubs. Big hotels, like the Sierra Radisson Plaza, and vacation residences, mainly condominiums, stand around a magnificent, world-class pleasure-craft port with all the modern amenities. Although Nuevo Vallarta is fairly far from the centre of Puerto Vallarta, you can get downtown by taxi *(100 pesos, about $12 US)* or bus. The bus service is almost as fast, once the bus gets onto the highway *(6 pesos or about $0.80 US)*.

  ## BEACHES ACCESSIBLE BY BOAT

Boat service is frequent to Yelapa, Playa Quimixto, Playa Las Ánimas and Chimo. You can't get to any of these beaches by land.

The **Playa Las Ánimas** ★★★ (Beach of Spirits) lies in the heart of a charming fishing village. Beneath the *palapas* of the restaurants set up on this magnificent beach, you can dine on fabulously fresh fish and seafood.

The **Playa Quimixto** ★★★ is ideal for visitors who want to combine swimming with hiking. You can even go for a pony ride here. There is a pretty waterfall about a half-hour's walk from the beach.

The small **Playa Majahuitas** was virtually unknown until quite recently. Situated between Quimixto and Yelapa, it lies at the foot of the hills covered by a lush tropical forest. The place is protected, and agencies organize few excursions there. **Majahuitas Resort** (see p 129) owns the property and offers stays in small bungalows.

**Yelapa** ★★★ is an attractive fishing hamlet. These days, mobs of visitors flock to this riverside beach, along which stand restaurants, a rustic hotel (Hotel Laguna de Yelapa) and kiosks with watersports equipment. Some can even supply instructors. When there, follow the river upstream on foot or horseback to view the waterfalls. If you don't like crowds, avoid this beach!

The little village of **Chimo**, on the southern tip of the bay, was and remains unknown to the vast majority of tourists. This little Eden boasts several beaches hidden along the coast. Property

SIGHTS AND BEACHES

developers and contractors are now there, however, and there is some talk of ecotourism development and adventure tourism.

## AROUND PUERTO VALLARTA

### South

The area south of Puerto Vallarta is worth exploring, both for its beautiful landscapes and its colourful, charming villages. To the south, the road follows the contours of the coast to **Mismaloya** (see p 96) and **Boca de Tomatlán** (see p 96) before penetrating into the verdant forests of the Sierra Madre. This route is lined with soaring cliffs and winding rivers. The higher you go the drier the climate; the road runs through mountains of pine forests to the village of **El Tuito**. Here *raicilla* is produced, a *maguey*-based alcohol similar to tequila. The Nuevo Restaurant Nena is also located here (see p 151)

### North

In the State of Nayarit, north of Puerto Vallarta, the land around Bay of the Flags (*Bahía de Banderas*) is rather flat, but pleasant nonetheless. **Jarretadera**, the first village along the way, is nothing extraordinary, except for its rustic simplicity. A winding dirt road leads through a cluster of dilapidated houses, into the village's residential centre where there is a beautiful view of the sea and a peaceful beach. Some people from other parts of North America have made their homes here.

The region is largely agricultural; several plantations have developed here due to the well-irrigated and fertile soil. Mango, avocado, papaya, sugar cane and corn are some of the vegetables harvested. The people live in the various towns and villages scattered throughout the region. Every Sunday, the town of **San Vicente** hosts the *charreada*, a traditional Mexican rodeo very popular in Jalisco State. It is quite a show, but might not appeal to those against cruelty to animals. Though the *charreada* is part of the local culture, one cannot help but cringe at the sight of a young frightened horse running frantically away from its rider who is determined to control it. Even worse, the rider uses his lasso and whip to overpower the horse, then ties the lasso around the horse's legs and drags him down to the ground in triumph. The audience is mostly made up of locals, but even they are becoming tired of this cruel form of entertainment called *paseo de la muerte*, and are beginning to take measures against it.

In the centre of the tranquil village of San Vincente, opposite the church, is a shady park and the public market. Around the park there are many *taquerías* where the male population gathers.

By travelling further inland, you will reach **San Jose del Valle**, an important agricultural community in the region. On its main street stands an impressive colonial-style church whose masterful architecture likens it to a cathedral. Every Sunday, locals go to the municipal park to watch football games between regional teams. San Jose del Valle also has the unfortunate reputation of being a brothel-town.

The national road 200, which runs along the bay until La Cruz de Huanacaxtle, passes through **Bucerias ★**. Here, restaurants, *taquerias*, terraces, cafés, stores and businesses line this long road, making it the town's main street. The neighbouring streets are lined with even more shops and are also full of street vendors unloading their wagons full of jewels, crafts, clothing, etc. Many restaurants, mostly serving fish and seafood, a pizzeria and a few terraces border the beach. Many Americans have establlished residences here. A small city, Bucerias offers a quiet escape from the bustling excitement of Puerto Vallarta, yet with all the tourist services: supermarkets, clinics, travel agencies, dry cleaners, etc.

From Bucerias, the national road forks off. The road to the left follows the coast and passes two fishing villages, **La Cruz de Humancaxtle** and **El Anclote**, as well as several beaches: **Manzanilla, Destiladeras, Paraíso Escondido** and **El Anclote** (see p 98). It finally leads to the Punta de Mita, a headland that juts out into the Pacific. Unfortunately, access to it is temporarily blocked due to the construction of a huge hotel complex that will undoubtably mar its singular natural beauty. The road to the right leads through large cactus (*nopales*), mango, avocado and papaya plantations. These plantations can be visited and are easily accessible by bus (*10 pesos; service*

**SIGHTS AND BEACHES**

*every 20 min).* Continuing down the 200, a little past Bucerias and the Sierra Madre valley is **Saylita ★★**, another magnificent beach on the Pacific frequented mostly by a young crowd consisting of families and couples, gay and straight. Here, instead of big hotel complexes obstructing the view, are villas, bungalows, houses and studios for rent, some of which have direct access to the beach. On the south of Bucerias beach, is a pretty little hotel (see p 130) on the rocks that blends marvellously into the surroundings. On the north part of the beach, the sea washes over two kilometres of sand in long, repetitive waves, creating a lulling and peaceful retreat for sun bathers and surfers. Vendors also roam the beaches of Bahía de Banderas, but are few compared to the crowds of tourists who flock here. The gourmet restaurant, Don Pedro, is in the middle of Bucerias beach (see p 150). There is a great view of the surroundings from its terrace. There is some lovely scenery on the way to **San Francisco ★**, the next stop after Bucerias, also known as San Panho. Surfers flock here to brave the waves considered to be the best in the region. The road stops by an attractive spot that leads to the sea through a row of *palapas*. The road is lined with restaurants with terraces, one of which is a small bar with big-screen TVs geared toward a sports-loving American clientele, and a monkey on a leash in the corner, a truly sorry sight. From the centre of San Francisco, a road that goes to Costa Azul Adventure Resort, an amazing place with luxurious villas and studios, where many outdoor activities (surfing, kayaking, fishing, cycling, hiking, etc.) can be practised. Further along, the same road penetrates a dense tropical forest through a steep and uneven landscape which, at certain points, offers magnificent views of the sea. Nestled deep in the forest are some rich private properties.

---

## East

---

High in the mountains, 62 km from Puerto Vallarta, **San Sebastián del Oeste** sits in the tropical forest. Once a prosperous silver-mining town with a population of 25,000, it is now little more than a small village whose 400 residents live peacefully amid unspoiled nature. By following the mountain road, you get to a secondary road leading to **Talpa de Allende**, perched in a valley at an altitude of more than 1,200 m. *Rollo*

## A Day in the Life of Puerto Vallarta, as Experienced by the Authors

Visitors to Puerto Vallarta kick back into vacation mode during the peak tourist seasons, but local residents never do. Most of them work in the hotel industry or for municipal maintenance services; and start their jobs early in the day. By sunrise, the streets are alive with these city dwellers. Even before groups of tidy school children line up in neat rows for their first classes, brigades of workers are on the job. Armed with brooms, brushes, pails and cloths, they set about the big daily cleaning. They change bedding in rooms and studio apartments, clean flower boxes on terraces, polish the steps on the staircases leading to hotels and wash the sidewalks with water. By the time a visitor stirs from bed, Puerto Vallarta has been scrubbed from top to bottom. A distinct odour of detergent permeates the entire city, to be gradually replaced by aromas emanating from early-opening cafés.

It's almost 8am. Joggers of all ages are staying in shape by running on the sandy beaches. They have to run now, because in half an hour the sun will be too hot and strong for any form of exercise. On the Playa de los Muertos pier, a handful of early risers watch the last fishing boats disappear into the distance. In another hour, by around 9am, the first swimmers and sun-worshippers will begin arriving on this beach in the heart of the city, some toting big shoulder-bags and others just a bottle of tanning lotion. At La Palapa, one of the innumerable restaurants along Playa de los Muertos, boss Alberto Perez Gonzales gives his staff directives for the day as one of his waiters, Hectoro, busies himself setting up tables and lounge chairs on the already-hot sand. On the terrace overlooking the beach, under the shade thrown by trellises of coconut leaves, the first patrons arrive to watch the parade of people and appease their hunger, whether with a hearty local *desayuno* or an American breakfast.

By 10am, the beach is swarming with people, a motley, cramped crowd whose apparel, however skimpy, is in stunningly loud taste. They battle for territorial rights over *palapas*, tiny tables or, failing that, a chair. Those who miss out must content themselves with whatever space there is on the sand. Now the beach is a mosaic of towels, as colourful as their owners.

Guards, who always patrol in pairs, navigate calmly among the bodies offered up to the sun, making sure everything is orderly. The regulars, North Americans who have fled winter back home and are known locally as "snowbirds", settle in a little farther along, separated from the crowd and the parade of vendors hawking their wares to beach-goers.

At 10:30am, newspaper vendors arrive to shout out the headlines from the Puerto Vallarta and Guadalajara papers, and from the big American dailies. By now the beach throbs with fevered activity, somewhere between a fair and a bazaar. Meanwhile, far above this human anthill, a parasailor is doing his thing. Propped on a seat attached to a sail linked by cable to a motor boat that's cruising up and down the bay, he will soar between heaven and earth for 20 minutes before landing safely on an unoccupied portion of the beach. This is a very popular activity among visitors not afraid of heights! All day long, a parade of adventurers will take their place on the contraption.

Back on the ground, in a scene repeated 1,000 times over, beach vendors hawk all manner of wares, from handicrafts to banana cakes. Around 11am, they start selling skewers of shrimp or fish.

It's 11am. Moving from one crowd of tourists to another, a ventriloquist makes his dummy sing Mexican folk songs. When coins begin dropping into his moneybag, the marionette bows and offers profuse thanks. His act is followed by groups of two or three singers and musicians, and sometimes entire families, eager to perform for the crowd. The same entertainers will appear on café and restaurant terraces later in the day.

At 11:30, the gringos' colour has changed from white to scarlet, caused by the cumulative effects of either the sun or too many beers, margaritas and rum-and-Cokes! At exactly noon, the waiters at La Palapa take their first orders.

The sun is high in the sky. A giant of a man with a protruding chest, carrying a heavy box on a shoulder strap, appears suddenly. It's "Mr. Choco Banana", come to work the beach. He is selling frozen bananas that have been dipped in chocolate flavoured with coffee liqueur and then rolled in crushed nuts. He finds plenty of takers. He's scarcely left the beach when a frail, elderly woman, her face lined by time, takes his place, but it's a bit late for "Mrs. Choco Banana".

Very few people leave the beach before late afternoon. But by the time the waiters at La Palapa start setting up torches in the sand to provide light during *cena* (dinner), the beach is virtually deserted.

*de guayaba*, the famous guava pâté popular in Mexico, is produced in this farming village of 7,000. A cathedral dedicated to the Virgin of Talpa stands in the centre of the village. Nearby is a cluster of motels and a Spanish *hacienda*, which has been converted into a hotel and serves as a departure point for horseback or bicycle tours. Although both villages are accessible by road, it is best to fly to them *(Mon to Fri; Vallarta airport ☎1-12-04)*.

Night driving is dangerous. Various animals and livestock cross the road and it's hard to spot them in time in the dark. If you must drive at night, stay on the main roads. Secondary roads are not practical; by sticking to the main roads, you can get help faster in case of a breakdown or other problems. Furthermore, it's important to respect the speed limit, as the highway is patrolled.

Note, too, that there have been numerous reports of thefts by "highway robbers", who, after stopping a car, relieve its occupants of all their money, jewellery, etc. Reportedly, some of these "good Samaritans" are eager to offer help if you have a flat tire, even in broad daylight!

SIGHTS AND BEACHES

# OUTDOOR ACTIVITIES

**M**ountain treks, deep-sea fishing, golf, scuba diving, camping, cycling and swimming are just a few of the many activities to be enjoyed in Puerto Vallarta and its vicinity. The state of Jalisco is an Eden that is unmatched in North America, and it boasts countless spots conducive to all manner of sports so you can plan your activities according to your tastes. Whether you're on your own, a couple, part of a group or with your family, the Puerto Vallarta area offers something for everyone.

 SPORTFISHING

Sportfishing is a favourite activity of visitors to Puerto Vallarta and other Mexican resorts. Here's a deep-sea fishing calendar based on to the seasons:

January, February and March: Pacific mackerel, roosterfish, tuna.
April: Pacific mackerel, roosterfish.
May: Pacific mackerel, roosterfish, sailfish.
June and July: sailfish.
August: black mackerel, blue mackerel, striped mackerel.

September, October, November and December: black mackerel, blue mackerel, striped mackerel, sailfish, tuna, kingfish.

You can get all the information you need on the necessary fishing permits, as well as a list of charter firms specializing in this kind of trip, by inquiring at a travel agency or at the Puerto Vallarta tourism bureau *(Mon to Sat 9am to 9pm; Plaza Principal, northeast side, ☎2-02-42)*.

One of the best fishing charter outfits is:

Raúl Gutiérrez
Paseo Díaz Ordaz and 31 de Octubre
*(at the far north end of the Malecón)*
☎2-12-02.

 DIVING

The most spectacular diving sites are around Islas Marietas, Quimixto and the rocky islets of Los Arcos. Information and equipment rentals are available at:

Chico's Dive Shop
770-5 Paseo Díaz Ordaz
*(across from the Malecón)*
☎2-18-95 or 2-54-39
≈2-18-97

Nuevo Vallarta
☎(329) 7-03-44

Vallarta Adventure
☎1-06-57 or 1-06-58

Vallarta Divers
17, Marina del Rey
☎1-04-92

Twin Dolphins Dive Center
7-A-B, Marina del Rey
Marina Vallarta
☎1-24-92

 BICYCLING

Cycling has become so popular in Puerto Vallarta that agencies now offer myriad guided tours in the neighbouring mountains, along the Río Cuale's scenic trails and to surrounding villages. Some packages include meals. An expedition usually lasts about 5 hours *($30 US; Sun Bike, Basilio Badillo no. 381, ☎2-00-80, ask for Mr. Hugo López).*

Bike Mex
361, Guerrero
☎3-16-80

## HORSEBACK RIDING

**Rancho El Ojo de Agua** *(180 pesos or $25 US; every day 10am to 1pm and 3pm to 6pm; Cerrada del Cardenal no. 227, Fraccionamiento Aralias; ☎4-06-07 or 4-82-40, ask for Marie)* specializes in renting out horses and offers guided trips into the interior and through the magnificent mountains along the coast. Some excursions last up to five days and go to remote villages in the western Sierra Madre. **El Charro** *(☎4-01-14)* offers similar services.

The smaller **Rancho Manolo** *(km 12, Carretera a Barra de Navidad, Mimaloya, to the right under the bridge; reservations ☎2-36-94 or 8-00-18)* offers horse rentals *(140 pesos or $20 US for 3 hours)* or guided treks ranging from 3 to 9 hours *(450 pesos or $60 US for 9 hours)* in the Río Mismaloya valley. The route leads to the exquisite tropical parks of Chino's Paraíso and El Edén. The river is a series of waterfalls and water pools. Although you'll see lots of people swimming, we advise against it.

The horseback trek also takes you to where the Mexican film *Predator*, an extravaganza loaded with special effects, was shot, this explains the helicopter near the restaurant.

You can also rent horses on Olas Altas street, near the pier on Playa de los Muertos.

## GOLF

The very popular **Marina Vallarta Golf Club** offers a world-class course. Located near Marina Vallarta's big hotels, this club offers all the latest services and equipment. Discounts are available to guests staying at some of the hotels near the course *(reservations: ☎1-00-73 or 1-0545)*. Another 18-hole course, the less select and more modest **Flamingos Golf Club**, is located near Nuevo Vallarta. There is a free shuttle service from the Sheraton Buganvilias hotel, daily at 7:30am and 10am with returns at 1pm and 4pm. The course has a restaurant, bar and pool *($43 US, $33 US after 3pm; ☎8-02-80 or 8-06-06)*.

 WATER PARK

The **Mayan Palace** water complex *(every day, 11am to 7pm; Paseo de la Marina Sur, Marina Vallarta, ☎1-11-55 or 1-15-00 ext. 608)* is in Marina Vallarta, across from the Vidafel hotel. The complex houses numerous slides, including two that feature inflatables. One section is reserved for young children. There are also a pool and a restaurant. The water park is a good place to cool off, but a word of warning: avoid swallowing any water or getting it up your nose, because it's definitely not distilled!

 DAY CRUISES

With assistance from the states of Jalisco and Nayarit, as well as from the private sector, the Mexican government has launched a major tourism development initiative throughout the Bahía de Banderas region.

The area around Puerto Vallarta abounds with gorgeous sites for swimming and picnicking. The best cruises take you to the isolated beaches of **Yelapa**, **Quimixto** and **Playa Las Ánimas**, all three of which are accessible only by water.

Various firms offer round-trip packages, including breakfast and lunch, for between 150 and 250 pesos (roughly $20 to $32 US), with a stop at the Los Arcos islets in the national marine park, where you can rent diving equipment. The boats depart daily at 9am from the harbour and returns around 4pm.

Information on tours and cruises to the three islands is available at most hotels and travel agencies in Puerto Vallarta. The following are some of the main companies offering cruise tours:

**Princesa Vallarta** *(every day 9:30am to 4:30pm;* ☎*4-47-77)*. Explore the sea bed of Los Arcos and Las Ánimas.

**Bora Bora** *(every day 9:30am to 5pm; Carretera Aeropuerto, km 3.5, Hotel Vallarta beach,* ☎*4-36-80 or 4-54-84)*. Los Arcos, Quimixto and Las Ánimas.

**Marigalante** *(every day 9am to 5pm,* ☎*3-03-09 or 3-16-62)*. Cruise on a replica of a Spanish galleon to Los Arcos, Las Ánimas and Quimixto.

**Curceros Princesa** *(every day 9am to 4pm; Paseo de las Garzas no. 100-B,* ☎*4-47-77)*. Los Arcos, Las Ánimas, Quimixto, Majahuitas, Yelapa and Islas Marietas.

**Buenaventura** *(every day 9am to 5pm; Paseo Díaz Ordaz no. 770-21,* ☎*3-03-09)*. Los Arcos, Quimixto and Las Ánimas.

**Cielito Lindo** *(every day 9:30am to 4pm;* ☎*2-18-77 or 2-43-37)*. Explore Los Arcos and Las Ánimas.

**Ecotour** *(Ignacio L. Vallarta no. 243,* ☎*2-66-06)*. Whale watching, kayaking and windsurfing excursions.

**Marigalante** *(every day 9am to 5pm;* ☎*3-03-09 or 3-16-62)*. On a replica of a Spanish galleon — Los Arcos, Las Ànimas and Quimixto.

**Vallarta Adventure** *(9am to 4pm; Marina Golf, office 13, Marina Vallarta,* ☎*1-06-57 or 1-06-58)*. Visit to the Islas Marietas, scuba diving and whale watching.

**Princesa Vallarta** *(every day 9:30am to 4:30pm;* ☎*4-47-77)*. Exploring the seabeds of Los Arcos and Las Ànimas.

**Sea Mi amor** *(every day 10am to 4pm; Lazaro Cárdenas, no. 536,* ☎*2-41-16)*. Los Arcos, Las Ánimas and Quimixto.

**Viva Tours** *(Carretera Aeropuerto, Terminal Marítimo,* ☎*4-04-10, 4-80-03 or 4-80-26)*. Discover the bay on board a trimaran. Day and night cruises.

**Sunset Cruises** *(*☎*4-47-77)*. Sunset cruises along the bay.

OUTDOORS

You can also take a water-taxi at the Rosita hotel *(at the north end of the Malecón, 11:30am)*, the Los Muertos beach pier *(10:30am or 11am)* or Boca de Tomatlán *(4pm or 5:30pm)*. It is best to check the schedules the night before your trip. It will cost between 100 and 120 pesos ($12 to $15 US) for the return trip.

The **Islas Marietas**, an ornithological marine reserve, lie south of Punta de Mita. The area is very popular with divers because of its superb underwater grottos and resident colonies of dolphins and giant manta rays. You might also see grey whales come here to breed between February and April. Most tours offer different activities: tours of the island, kayaking and diving, etc. Some packages include meals. For more information, contact a travel agency (prices range from $40 to $70 US).

Other available boat trips include a sunset tour of the bay *(Marigalante ☎3-03-09 or Princesa Vallarta ☎4-47-77)* or a dinner cruise.

L odging options are divided into five price categories, listed below. Rates quoted are for a room for two people, including a 15% tax but not including breakfast. "All-inclusive" means the price covers all meals and drinks as well as the room. Please also refer to the table of symbols at the front of the book.

| | | |
|---|---|---|
| $ | = | $30 US or less |
| $$ | = | $30 to $50 US |
| $$$ | = | $50 to $70 US |
| $$$$ | = | $70 to $100 US |
| $$$$$ | = | $100 US and up |

Most hotels cited are located in specific neighbourhoods, and together they account for a good part of the tourist lodging in Puerto Vallarta. The northern part of the city is full of places to stay; this is where you'll find the main hotels. There are rows upon rows of hotels on Paseo de Las Palmas and in Marina Vallarta, including many of the most upscale resorts in town. Downtown, more modest hotels offer rooms or studio apartments right in the heart of Puerto Vallarta giving visitors a real taste of what life is like here. Other luxurious hotels are to be found in the south, either on the hillsides or near beaches. In Nuevo Vallarta, most hotels are of the all-inclusive; vacation packages offered by travel agencies which often include the cost of the hotel stay as well as the air fare and airport pick-up and drop-off.

 # THE OLD TOWN

Most of Puerto Vallarta's budget hotels are found in the neighbourhoods along the Río Cuale. These are a good bet for travellers who really want to experience "Vallartian" life. In addition to being extremely well maintained, these lodgings boast a great location — close to the beach and the best restaurants, in an area crowded with shops and cafés.

## North of the Río Cuale

Avenida México, the main thoroughfare in northern Puerto Vallarta, is as busy as it is noisy. Moreover, its parallel traffic lanes and neighbouring streets alike are not all paved, the air is extremely polluted in dry weather. This area is nevertheless a residential zone with a few restaurants, shops, a cinema, a supermarket (Plaza Ley), a Pemex gas station as well as a variety of little street stalls. A little below and slightly set back from Avenida México's anarchic urban sprawl stands **Hotel El Pescador** *($-$$$; pb, ≡/⊗, ≈, tv, ☎; Paraguay no. 1117, at Calle Uruguay, ☎2-21-69 or 2-18-84, for reservations in Mexico 01-800-23-610-00, ≈3-20-00)*. The lobby leads to a lovely terrace that looks out onto Playa Camarones. The rooms are air-conditioned, and the best ones have a balcony with an ocean view as well as two queen-size beds. The others, some of which can accommodate up to six people, are more modest and overlook the street.

Tucked away in the heart of the northern residential area, away from the hotel zone, in another somewhat disparate setting, are the **Coral Suites** *($$; pb, ≡, ⊗, tv, ☎, K, ≈; Sierra Aconcagua no. 140, ☎2-40-84 or 2-40-74)*. This renovated hotel borders one side of a long narrow courtyard, which is both a garden and a parking lot. In the middle, there is a covered terrace with tables and chairs, and the pool is nearby. The place has been tastefully renovated, inside has been decorated with attractive colours and Mexican ceramic tiles bearing flower motifs. The rooms have kitchens modern

## Casa Kimberly:
### Elizabeth Taylor and Richard Burton's Love Nest

In January 1964, Elizabeth Taylor visited Puerto Vallarta. Why did she come here—to keep an eye on her love, actor Richard Burton, who was on location filming *Night of the Iguana*, to discuss making movies together or to quietly enjoy a two-month "pre-honeymoon" before their Montreal wedding? Puerto Vallarta, a small sleepy fishing village then unknown to journalists, would offer Burton and Taylor, before their double divorce, a love nest. They settled in a large three-storey tiled-roof estate with patios enclosed by elegant wrought-iron gates and terraces sheltered from the hot sun by lemon trees, coconut palms, papaya and banana trees. The lovely little Venetian-style pink-stucco bridge (somewhat reminiscent of the Pont des Soupirs in Paris) that spans narrow Calle Zaragoza in the Gringo Gulch district (in the high town, behind the cathedral) leads to other rooms of the estate. However spacious, the romantic hideaway was not large enough for the two actors, Taylor's children, the dogs, cats, birds, luggage and staff. The couple liked Casa Kimberly so much that they bought the place and returned several times. Their presence largely contributed to the seaside resort's popularity.

**Casa Kimberly** *($50 to $85 in season, 50% discount off-season; bkfst incl.; Calle Zaragoza no. 445, ☎2-13-36)* has been converted into a bed-and-breakfast since Elizabeth Taylor and Richard Burton stayed here. Sleeping in the same room formerly occupied by the stormy couple would really make your stay more of an experience, for the villa remains a not-to-be-missed attraction. The walls of its spacious living rooms are adorned with scores of photographs depicting the happy times spent here by these young lovers.

furnishings such as a stove, refrigerator, and kitchen table located behind a counter. The queen-size bed is in an alcove making the place quite spacious and bright. Next to the bed is a sofa bed for an extra guest. The closest beach is only a few minutes away, behind the major seaside hotels on the other side of Boulevard Francisco Medina Ascencio. Warm welcome and very friendly staff.

In the heart of downtown Vallarta, beside the Río Cuale and near what is known as the "first bridge", **Hotel Encino** *($$-$$$; pb, ≡, ≈, K, tv, ☎, ≈, ℜ; Juárez no 122, ☎2-00-51 or 01-800-3-26-36 for reservations in Mexico, ⌐2-25-73)* offers good daily and monthly rates. The rooms are well kept and the balconies, looking out on an interior courtyard graced with a lovely fountain, allow guests to enjoy the refreshing breeze. Moreover, a few tables and armchairs are set out in the courtyard so that guests may take advantage of this inviting oasis. The hotel also boasts a rooftop restaurant and a poolside terrace with a lovely view of the city, the mountains and the sea. Comfortable suites are housed in the adjacent building. These one- or two-room suites have a kitchenette and a living room that also serves as a dining area. Though not air conditioned, the rooms are sufficiently ventilated by ceiling fans and have sliding doors that open onto a streetfront balcony.

🦐 The **Rosita** hotel *($$-$$$; pb, ≡, ⊗, ≈, ℜ, tv; Calle Paseo Díaz Ordaz no. 901, ☎3-21-85 or 3-21-42)*, at the far north end of the Malecón, stands peaceably amid the surrounding hubbub. Its 90 rooms are basic and clean. It also has several more comfortable suites, and the staff is very cordial. The terrace and pool, adequately shaded by palm trees, overlook the ocean. The hotel is next door to Puerto Vallarta's fish market. It's also the departure point for water-taxis to Yelapa, Quimixto and Las Ánimas beaches.

## South of the Río Cuale

Next to the very popular Café de Olla, the **Yasmin Hotel** *($-$$; pb, ⊗, #; Calle Basilio Badillo no. 168, ☎2-00-87)* mainly attracts young travellers who don't want the basic amenities. It looks like an American motel, with rooms on two floors and unadorned white brick walls. A few tables and chairs are set up in the complex's inner courtyard, which has almost no shade.

The **Vista al Oceano Suites** *($-$$$; pb, ≡, ⊗, ≈, ⊗, K, km 1.2 Carretera a Barra de Navidad, ☎3-07-08)* is located atop a hill, but unfortunately the view of the ocean is partially blocked by the imposing Tropicana hotel. On the other hand, the hotel's 10 rooms of various sizes are sheltered by the hill from the traffic. The suites are inviting and each has a balcony.

The **Paco Paco - Descanso del Sol** *($-$$$$; pb, ≡, ⊛, ≈, K; Calle Pino Suárez no. 583, ☎2-02-77 or 800-936-3646, ⌐2-67-67)* was recently opened by the owners of Paco Paco, the most popular gay bar in town. This hillside hotel offers well-maintained rooms and suites with balconies.

The **Vallarta Cora** hotel *($$; pb, ≡, ⊛, K; Pilitas no. 174, ☎3-28-15, coragay@pvnet.com.mx, contact Mario Lavoie)* is a favourite with the North American gay community. Though it is situated near the city centre, it is quietly located at the end of an alley set back from Calle Pilitas. Each room comes with a kitchenette and living room and is attractively decorated with warm- and bright-coloured ceramic tiles, and the bathrooms are large. What's more, the famous Playa Los Muertos is only some hundred metres away.

The **Posada de Roger** *($$; pb, ≡, ⊛, ≈, ℜ, K, tv, ☎; Calle Basilio Badillo no. 237, at the corner of Calle Ignacio L. Vallarta, ☎2-08-36 or 2-06-39, ⌐1-11-48)* offers rooms with balconies overlooking busy Los Muertos beach; at this hotel, you're in the heart of the action. The interior courtyard boasts a lovely garden. The pool is on the rooftop terrace. This well-maintained, attractive hotel has an excellent reputation and offers monthly rentals.

The **Posada Río Cuale** *($$; pb, ≡, ⊛, ≈, ℜ, tv; Aquiles Serdán no. 242, ☎322-2-04-50, 2-09-14 or 2-11-48)*, at the corner of busy Calle Ignacio L. Vallarta, is a delightful hotel with 20 rooms, some of which open onto a beautifully laid-out patio. Its bar-restaurant near the pool attracts a mellow crowd.

Olas Altas, which runs parallel to the sea, is a very busy thoroughfare. At day's end, tourists take this street from the beach to the downtown restaurants, bars and shops. **Hotel Alegre** *($$; pb, ≡, ⊛, ℜ, tv, ≈; Francisca Rodríguez no. 168, ☎⌐2-47-93)* is located on a quiet street off of Olas Atlas and a small flowered patio and a swimming pool add to its tranquility. The peaceful place welcomes many American vacationers who take advantage of its rates, more affordable than the other hotels around. The rooms are modest and sparsely decorated, even though it was renovated two years ago.

The **Brisas del Mar** *($$-$$$; pb, ≡, ⊛, ≈, K; Privada Abedus no. 10, ☎2-18-00 or 2-18-21, ⌐2-67-07)* affiliated with the

Tropicana hotel (see further below). The hotel is not of recent construction, but its suites are very well kept by a kind and courteous staff who deserve their tip. Below, on the large terrace with a swimming pool that overlooks the sea, is a newly added *palapa*-roofed bar. Unfortunately, it's the same story every night: loud music blares from the bar late into the night obliging guests to close their doors when it would be so much more pleasant to listen to the sound of the waves washing up on shore! The situation soon becomes intolerable since the sounds of *fiestas* from neighbouring establishments fill the air virtually every night. The only way to fall asleep is to the din of old, humming air-conditioners. Next to the hotel, a long flight of stairs well shaded by bougainvillea and tropical fruit trees and bordered by charming houses, leads to the sea and the lower town. The first street on the right, at the foot of the stairs, leads to the different downtown districts. The hotel offers special weekly and monthly rates; the best rates are through tour operators.

**Hotel Suites Emperador** *($$-$$$; pb, ≈, ⊗, K; Amapas no. 115, at the corner of Rodolfo Gómez, ☎2-33-29, ≠2-33-29)* is now run by sisters Cornejo, Liney and Alexandra, who plan on renovating the place, which though still very clean, is somewhat the worse for wear. The establishment is very quiet. The one-, two- or three-room suites come with either a king-size bed or two double or single beds; the bigger suites also come with a sofa bed. Each unit has a private balcony overlooking the street, which is very busy during the day. Guests must go up to the terrace for a lovely view of the sea, partly hidden in part by the high-rise hotels and apartment buildings across the street.

The **Tropicana** *($$-$$$; pb, ≈, ⊗, ≈, ℜ, ☎; Calle Amapas no. 214, ☎2-09-12, ≠2-67-37)* is an imposing, austere building with 220 rooms that make a concrete wall facing the ocean. The hotel is affiliated with many travel agencies and offers some interesting packages. Although the building is architecturally boring, its balconies at least overlook the ocean, which makes it a pleasant place just the same. The room decor is modest, but the welcome is warm despite the size of the place.

The vibrantly coloured **Puerto Vallarta Beach Hotel** *($$-$$$; pb, ≈, ⊗, ≈, ℜ, ℝ, tv, ☎; Malecón y Almendro no. 4,*

☎2-50-40, *or* 2-21-76, ⁼2-50-40) is the last in the string of hotels along the beach, making it an oasis of peace. There's very little car traffic in the area and guests can soak up the restful atmosphere by swimming in the roof-top pool next to the restaurant or by taking part in various activities on the beach below. Sixteen of the 40 rooms have balconies with unobstructed ocean views. Every one of the rooms, warmly decorated with painted ceramic tiles, display the richness of this prolific Mexican art. Worthwhile accommodation packages are available here through travel agencies.

Two blocks from sea, at the end of a cul-de-sac, stands the **Los Arcos Vallarta Hotel** *($$-$$$$; pb, ≡, ⊗, ≈, K, ℝ, tv, ☎; Manuel M. Diéguez no. 171, ☎2-17-12, 2-15-83 or 800-648-2403, ⁼2-24-18),* formerly the Fontana del Mar. The small hotel of Spanish-influenced architecture houses 40 newly renovated, lightly furnished rooms in decorated white tones. The lovely royal-blue bedspreads and cushions add a nice touch to the off-white beds and armchairs. A few rooms also have a kitchenette and balcony. Like many other establishments, this one offers a rooftop terrace and swimming pool, whence guests have a lovely view of the city and the bay. The hotel shares the same beach as the neighbouring Playa Los Arcos hotel.

The **Gloria del Mar - Maxime's Suites** *($$$; pb, ≡, K; Amapas no. 114, ☎2-51-43, ⁼2-67-37)* rents out modest but well-equipped studio apartments. The site boasts an attractive view of the ocean but none of the rooms have balconies. Furthermore, there's no pool; guests have to use the one at the Tropicana next door.

Built around a pool, with a superb terrace overlooking the beach, the **Playa Los Arcos** *($$$-$$$$; pb, ≡, ⊗, ≈, ℜ, ℝ, tv, ☎; Olas Altas no. 380, ☎2-15-83 or 800-684-2403, ⁼2-24-18)* has all the amenities of a luxury hotel: boutiques, a travel agency, medical services and water sports. Most of the rooms and studio apartments have a view of the sea.

Starting at the Puerto Vallarta Beach hotel, a low wall runs along the street topped by railings behind which stately trees spread their majestic branches. The wire-mesh doors open onto a long stairway leading to the **Plaza Corazón** *($$$ bkfst incl.; pb, ⊗; Amapas no. 326, ☎2-13-71),* a place where time seems to have stopped. Old-fashioned, though scarcely a few decades old (undoubtedly built in the 1970s), the establishment has a warm and intimate ambiance. The older part of the hotel is a three-storey structure built on the hillside. The 14 rooms on the two lower floors have two beds (a double and single), private entrances and many windows, and share a balcony with a splendid view. Though there is no air conditioning, the ceiling fans are just as good and the only way to fend off the mosquitos, particularly prevalent in the summer. Friday nights are *fiesta* time: the bar opens for cocktails then dinner is served in the dining room, where guests can listen to live music and dance to their hearts' content to *Latino* rhythms.

The southern part of Calle Amapas runs along the beach, then climbs sharply to join the road leading to Mismaloya. The **Meza del Mar** hotel *($$$-$$$$; pb, ≡, ☎, K, ℜ, X\*, ≈; Amapas no. 380, ☎2-48-88 or 888-694-0010, ↵2-23-08, club_meza⊗go2mexico.com)* is located in a bend off this winding road. Built on the cliffside, this hotel houses 127 rooms and suites. It offers all-inclusive packages and a lunch and dinner buffet is laid out on the magnificent terrace, where bands perform three times a week (Thursday, Friday and Saturday). Another restaurant, as well as a second swimming pool, await guests below, a stone's throw from Playa Los Muertos. The suites, the most luxurious and quiet of which are located below the terrace, consist of a living room, sometimes a kitchenette and a dining area, a balcony and one to two rooms, one of which offers an ocean view. The rooms come with a king-size bed or double bed and a single bed. The place is very well kept and offers all modern conveniences. Opt for a suite rather than a room when you make your reservation, because the latter are situated at the back of the building and offer no view whatsoever.

At the south end of the beach stands the **Vallarta Shores Hotel** *($$$-$$$$; pb, ≡, ⊛, K, ≈; El Malecón no. 400, ☎2-38-38 or 2-36-47, ↵2-39-39)*, an establishment with one-, two- and three-room suites, all of which boast a balcony or terrace. Large glass doors open onto the sea, allowing guests to enjoy the ocean breeze. A penthouse suite with private terrace and swimming pool is also available. The architecture of the place is a harmonious blend of brick, concrete and wood.

The **Los Arcos Suites** *($$$$; pb, ≡, π, tv, K, ≈; Manuel M. Diéguez no. 164, π2-07-00, 2-15-83 or 800-648-2403, ≈2-24-18, losarcos@playalosarcol.com)* are part of the Playa Los Arcos hotel complex. The suites, furnished in rustic Mexican style, come with a bedroom with a queen-size or king-size bed, a living-dining room area, and a private balcony overlooking an interior courtyard and a large, shaded swimming pool.

The **San Marino Plaza** *($$$$; pb, ≡, ⊛, ≈, ℜ, ℝ, tv; Calle Rodolfo Gómez no. 111, π2-15-55 or 2-30-50, ≈2-24-31)*, formerly the Oro Verde, looms over the Playa Los Muertos. It has 162 rooms and studio apartments with balconies; some have an ocean view. The rooms contain two queen-size beds as well as a table and colourful, hand-made wooden chairs. The bathrooms are brightened up by attractive Mexican tiles. Conference facilities are available. The hotel offers horseback treks, cruises, golf and tennis. The hotel is in a lively neighbourhood with plenty of services nearby.

The **Molino de Agua** *($$$$; pb, ≡, ⊛, ≈, ⊛, ℜ, ℝ; Calle Ignacio L. Vallarta no. 130, π2-19-57 or 2-19-07, ≈2-60-56)*, in a pretty garden setting at the edge of the Río Cuale, boasts one of the prettiest hotel properties in Puerto Vallarta. Peaceful despite its proximity to downtown, it offers a number of chalets nestled in a natural setting and several comfortable rooms near the water. It has a pool and a bar-restaurant.

## SOUTHERN PUERTO VALLARTA

This area, located 30 minutes from the airport and 10 minutes from downtown Puerto Vallarta, is perfect for those seeking tranquillity. The steep cliffs along the coast make the area quite isolated; there is hardly any residential development between the rich district of Conchas Chinas and Mismaloya. It is easy to get downtown from here; buses run regularly between Boca de Tomatlán and Puerto Vallarta.

 Visitors who love swimming in the ocean will find the **Camino Real** *($$$$$; pb, ≡, ⊛, ≈, ⊘, ℜ, ℝ, tv, π; Playa Las Estacas, π1-50-00 or 800-7-CAMINO)* much to their liking. And those who prefer pools will feel like they're swimming in the ocean, because the pool overlooks the beach. The hotel has a fine reputation and is particularly appreciated by its guests. The rooms are wonderfully comfortable and beautifully decorated by top Mexican designers. The site, in a sandy, deliciously secluded cove, is one of the most enchanting in Puerto Vallarta. But like the old Korean proverb says, a beautiful landscape holds no allure if there's nothing to eat. The Camino Real has that covered too; in fact it operates two restaurants. The first, La Brisa, serves up delicious fish and seafood; the other, even more renowned, La Perla, offers succulent French and Mexican cuisine plus a few classic international dishes (see p 146).

In the south central part of the Bahía des Banderas, **La Jolla de Mismaloya** *($$$$$; pb, ≡, ⊗, ≈, ⊘, ℜ, ℝ, tv, ☎; Playa Mismaloya, ☎8-06-60 or 800-322-2344, ⇒8-05-00)* contains more than 300 opulent suites with balconies and clear views of the ocean. Waterfalls splash amid its three huge pools, and the premises also contain a sauna, a massage studio and a physical fitness centre for guests' well-being. There are three restaurants from which to choose as well as three bars which offer a taste of more than 70 different brands of tequila. Travel and car rental agencies, a beauty salon, a massage studio, an exercise room and a game room line the main floor of the hotel facing the surrounding garden outside. Attractive all-inclusive packages are available.

On a beautiful sandy beach with lush vegetation, the **Blue Bay Club Puerto Vallarta** *($$$$$; pb, ≡, ⊗, ⊛, ≈, ⊘, △, ℜ, ℝ, tv, ☎, km 4, Carretera a Barra de Navidad, ☎1-55-00, ⇒1-51-05, pvr@bluebayresorts.com)* also offers all-inclusive packages. Even if you're not staying here, you can spend the day at the Blue Bay Club's "beachclub", with its big swimming pools, four bars and restaurants, one of which serves a day and evening buffet. The hotel's 300 rooms are of the utmost comfort and have big beds; the rooms facing the sea have balconies. There are also 76 studios with one or two bedrooms. Conference facilities and lots of activities.

The **Presidente Inter-Continental** *($$$$$; pb, ≡, ⊗, ⊛, ≈, ⊘, △, ℜ, ℝ, tv, ☎; km 8.5, Carretera a Barra de Navidad, ☎8-05-07, ⇒8-06-09)* is another five-star establishment offering reasonable all-inclusive packages. The hotel is nestled into a cliff on its own beach. This part of the coast is pretty isolated, and despite the road, serenity reigns here. Most of the rooms look out to sea.

## THE NORTHERN HOTEL ZONE

This is a major tourist centre, with rows of luxury hotels that all look the same. All the big properties listed below cater to their guests by offering tours and sporting activities. Most feature boutiques, kiosks and a variety of stores selling everyday and luxury goods. Some hotels also have medical clinics and day-care centres.

**Buenaventura** *($$$-$$$$$; pb; ≡, ≈, ⊘, ℜ, ℝ, tv, ☎; km 2.5, Avenida México no. 1301, ☎3-27-37, 2-37-37, 2-39-64 or 800-878-4484, ⇒2-08-70 or 2-35-46, buenaventura@puerto-vallarta.com)*. On the edge of the bustling Puerto Vallarta, this hotel is an oasis of tranquillity while still accessible to downtown by foot. As a four star hotel, it offers all of the expected amenities: over 225 comfortable rooms; boutiques; medical services; a travel agency; conference facilities, spa, etc. The restaurant and pool reach the beach side. Every Friday night, the Fiesta Mexicana hosts folk dancing and *mariachi* music on the poolside terrace.

Easily recognizable by its orange colour, the **Holiday Inn** *($$$-$$$$$; pb, ≡, ctv, ≈, ⊛, ⊘, △, ℜ, tv, ☎; Francisco Medina Ascencio, km 3.5; ☎6-17-00, 01-800-00-900 from Mexico or 800-HOLIDEX from the US, holipvr@vallegde.com.mx)* is the last hotel on Playa Parán before Río Ptitillal. It also offers all-inclusive packages and has 231 rooms with balconies and sea views. All the action here is centred around the swimming pool and restaurant, both which face the ocean and from where you can get a good view of the city and surrounding mountains. The friendly clientele is mostly Mexican.

Fifteen minutes from the airport and 5 minutes from downtown, the **Sheraton Buganvilias** *($$$$$; pb, ≡, ≈, ⊘, ℜ, ℝ, tv, ☎; Bulevar Francisco Medina Ascencio no. 999, ☎3-04-04 or 800-433-5451, ⇒2-05-00)* stands on the Las Glorias beach, known for its calm waters. The hotel has 650 comfortable rooms and its shopping hall is home to all manner of businesses. The property has an elegant meeting room and all the equipment necessary to stage an international convention.

The **Continental Plaza** *($$$$$; pb, ≡, ⊛, ≈, ⊘, ℜ, ℝ, tv, ☎; Playa Las Glorias, ☎4-01-23, 4-45-60 or 800-88CONTI, ⊷4-52-36)* has 424 rooms and lies just 10 minutes from the airport. The pool is next to the ocean and the hotel is close to downtown.

**Los Tules** *($$$$$; pb, ≡, ⊛, ≈, ℜ, ℝ, tv, ☎; km 2.5, Carretera al Aeropuerto, ☎4-54-25 or 800-553-2340, ⊷4-47-10)*, built in the Mediterranean style, rents out fully equipped rooms and studio apartments. It's located on one of the loveliest beaches on the Bahía des Banderas.

The **Qualton Club & Spa Vallarta** *($$$$$; pb, ≡, ctv, ☎, ⊛, ⊘, ◯, ℜ, ≈; Francisco Medina Ascencio, km 2.5, ☎4-44-46, ⊷4-44-45 or 4-44-47, qualton@pvnet.com.mx)* is one of the best thalassotherapy centres in Mexico. It offers many different activities and treatments including anti-stress massages, reflexology, yoga, hydrotherapy, algae baths, youth cures, aerobics, etc. Unfortunately, these treatments are not included in the all-inclusive packages. This 14-floor establishment has 220 rooms with private balconies and four studios with their own terraces and whirlpools facing the sea. The hotel encloses a big swimming pool on Las Glorias beach.

A few minutes by car from the airport and from downtown, the magnificent **Fiesta Americana** *($$$$$; pb, ≡, ≈, ⊘, ℜ, ℝ, tv, ☎; km 2.5, Bulevar Francisco M. Ascencio, ☎4-20-10 or 800-FIESTA1)* has an enormous lobby beneath a huge *palapa* with a splashing waterfall flanked by tropical plants. This extraordinary establishment has nearly 300 rooms, studio apartments and "presidential suites" (as the hotel calls them). It's also home to a veritable shopping centre that offers every imaginable service: a hairdressing salon, a day-care centre, a magazine shop, a medical clinic, clothing boutiques, etc.

At the **Kristal Vallarta** *($$$$$; pb, ≡, ⊛, ≈, ⊘, ℜ, ℝ, tv, ☎; Avenida de las Garzas, ☎4-02-02 or 800-231-9860, ⊷4-01-50 or 4-02-02, kristal@pvnet.com.mex)*, charming little bungalows are scattered about the sprawling site. The houses are set far enough apart to provide a fairly intimate atmosphere, and each has its own tiny pool, or, if you prefer, a giant bath.

 ## MARINA VALLARTA

This huge, luxurious hotel zone, into which developers have poured nearly half a billion US dollars, sprawls over more than 178 hectares. A boater's paradise, it is surrounded by condominiums and is bordered by a promenade lined with boutiques, art galleries, restaurants and cafés. The big hotels are some of the most beautiful on the Bahía de Banderas and are located along most of El Salado beach. Marina Vallarta is right near the airport and 10 minutes from downtown by bus or taxi.

Next door to the Marina golf course, the **Bel-Air** *($$$$$; pb, ≡, ◉, ≈, ℜ, ℝ, tv, ☎; Pelícanos, Marina Vallarta no. 311, ☎1-08-00 or 800-457-7676)* consists of 67 rooms and villas carefully decorated with fine detail. Surrounded by lush gardens, inviting terraces offer either a pool or whirlpool for relaxation and the bathrooms are renovated with elaborate marble floors. On display here is internationally known native artist Sergio Bustamente's collection of masks and sculptures.

With a prime location in the heart of the Marina, the **Marriott Casa Magna** *($$$$$; pb, ≡, ◉, ≈, ⊘, ℜ, ℝ, tv, ☎; Paseo de la Marina no. 5, ☎1-00-04 or 800-223-6388, ≈1-07-60)* is an enormous structure housing 433 rooms and 29 suites, a number of which have hot tubs. For those looking to get into shape, the hotel has a gym and three tennis courts. This property is 5 minutes by car from the airport, while downtown Puerto Vallarta is less than 10 minutes away by bus or taxi.

The **Westin Regina** *($$$$$; pb, ≡, ◉, ≈, ⊘, ℜ, ℝ, tv, ☎; Paseo de la Marina no. 205, ☎1-11-00 or 800-892-4580, ≈1-11-21, repue@westin.com)*, part of the international hotel chain, is surrounded by rich tropical vegetation. Besides the facilities, boutiques and other amenities offered by all the major hotels in Marina Vallarta, the Westin's 24-hour services include audiovisual equipment, a sauna, a massage studio and a host of daily activities for children and adults alike.

**Velas Vallarta** *($$$$$; pb, ≡, ⊗, ⊛, ≈, ⊘, △, ℜ, K, tv, ☎; Avenida Costera, no. 585, ☎1-00-91 or 800-VELASPV, ✆1-07-55, ventas@hotelvelas.com)* is another luxury hotel set back a little from the beach. The 361 richly decorated, one- to three-room studios have private terraces, some with swimming pools. Many activities are offered, such as cruises, horseback and bike rides, and as well guided tours of the area and golf packages for the nearby course.

## NUEVO VALLARTA

Nuevo Vallarta is home to a number of all-inclusive resorts, which have their own little "vacation colony" coast. Guests go with the flow at each place; some stay at the resort for their entire visit, apparently uninterested in seeing and experiencing anything else. More adventurous guests can sign on for the tours offered by most of the hotels.

 The **Club Oasis Marival** *($$$$; pb, ≡, ⊛, ≈, ⊘, ℜ, tv, ☎; Bulevar Nuevo Vallarta, Nuevo Vallarta, at the corner of Paseo de los Cocoteros, ☎329-7-01-00, ✆329-7-07-11 or in Montreal, ☎450-843-5777, ✆450-843-4581)* offers all-inclusive packages perfectly suited to small families looking for sporting activities in the pool and on the beach. Besides its supervised activity programs and a well-equipped playground for children, the hotel is a great place for horseback riding, bicycling, tennis, golf and lots of other outdoor activities. The 504 rooms and studios are located inside six buildings that each have a pool surrounded by lovely gardens and shady palm trees.

**Jack Tar Village** *($$$$; pb, ≡, ⊛, ≈, ⊘, ℜ, ℝ, tv, ☎; Paseo de los Cocoteros, Nuevo Vallarta, ☎329-8-02-26, ✆329-8-03-33)* also offers all-inclusive packages that include all the same features as neighbouring competitors. The shore on either side of the hotel is lined with large vacant properties, no doubt awaiting developers, and its beach throbs with all manner of activities.

The **Sierra Radisson** *($$$$; pb, ≡, ⊛, ≈, ⊘, ℜ, ℝ, tv, ☎; Paseo de los Cocoteros no. 19, Nuevo Vallarta, ☎329-7-13-00, ✆329-7-00-82)* has 350 rooms and offers all-inclusive packages. Like most properties in this area, the focus is on assorted sports and other outdoor activities. The buildings in the sprawling compound are laid out with wings in the shape of an X with half a slash missing.

The luxurious **Paradise Village** *($$$$$; pb, ≡, ⊛, ≈, ⊘, ℛ, K, tv, ☎; no. 001 Paseo de Los Cocoteros, Nuevo Vallarta, ☎329-7-07-70 or 800-995-5714, ⊷329-7-09-80)*, specializes in the ever-popular all-inclusive formula. The Mayan-style decor is dazzling. Each apartment of one, two or three rooms has its own terrace with a sea view. This place is popular with Europeans, who delight in the myriad activities available on the beach and in the pool area. The pools are beautifully designed, complete with waterfalls. At night, a wide variety of shows are presented.

 BEACHES ACCESSIBLE BY BOAT

## Majahuitas

This area, with its small beach scattered with fruit trees, is definitely the most tranquil in the region. The **Majahuitas Resort** *($$$$$; pb, ⊛, ℛ; Playa Majahuitas, ☎1-58-08, relax@cruzio.com)* is located here. Guests stay in bungalows with enough distance in between them to ensure peace and quiet. Electricity is provided by solar energy. Different activities are organized including volleyball, croquet, sailboarding, scuba diving and horseback riding. Prices include meals; a candle-light dinner is served on the terrace.

## Yelapa

This is a lost paradise — which alas has been rediscovered by thousands of North American tourists. Still, it's worth spending a day here or even staying overnight, to explore the natural setting and trek to the jungle waterfalls that plummet dozens of metres.

At the **Hotel Lagunita de Yelapa** *($; pb, K; Yelapa; ☎329-8-05-12 or 322-1-58-08)*, guests sleep under mosquito nets (indispensable!). At night, watch out for scorpions. Electricity and hot water are only turned on between 7am and

11pm. Hammocks hang here and there on the hotel terraces, so that guests can enjoy siestas. In later afternoon, after the last boat has gone, the place is a pleasant little haven of peace... which is not the case during the day, when wave after wave of tourists arrive and depart.

 AROUND PUERTO VALLARTA

## North

Just off the road from Bucerias facing the bay is pretty little **Vista Bahía** (*$$; pb, ≡, ⊗, K; Avenida de los Picos, no. 350, Playa de Huancaxtle, ☎329-8-02-30*). The establishment offers one- or two-room studios with kitchenettes and sofa-beds. The studios open onto a pretty terrace facing the beach. Weekly and monthly rentals are available.

## RESTAURANTS

**M**exican cuisine varies from one part of the country to another. Climatic conditions, whether in the mountains, in arid areas or on the coast, determine the kind of food served up in local establishments. Public markets still sell many products that were used by the indigenous peoples, including the Aztecs, who dwelt in the tropical part of the continent, in an area that runs from modern-day Mexico down to Peru, where potatoes, among other crops, were first grown. The Spaniards later introduced this tuber to the rest of the world, along with sweet potatoes, avocados, beans, corn, squash, pimentos, tomatoes, peppers, sunflowers, peanuts, pineapple, cocoa, vanilla and turkey, whose habitat spread as far up the Atlantic coast as New England. Other producers sell poultry, lamb, beef, pork and goat meat. The waters of the Bahía de Banderas supply Puerto Vallarta with fabulously fresh fish and seafood; be sure to sample some in local restaurants.

Prices in the categories below are for a meal for one person, including taxes and consisting of an appetizer, main dish, dessert and coffee (unless otherwise indicated). Drinks and tips are not included. As a rule, it's customary to leave a tip (*propina*) of between 10% and 15% in bars and restaurants. Menus don't always include taxes; in such cases, add 15 % to the meal price.

| $ | = | $5 US or under |
| $$ | = | $5 to $10 US |
| $$$ | = | $10 to $20 US |
| $$$$ | = | $20 to $30 US |
| $$$$$ | = | $30 US and up |

## PUERTO VALLARTA, GOURMET CITY

Though foreign, seasonal and permanent residents know and appreciate Puerto Vallarta's good restaurants, such is not the case for about 90% of those vacationing here. These tourists take advantage of packages offered to them through various European and (North, South and Central) American travel agencies. Even if these packages include accommodation and meals, visitors should not restrict themselves to this plan – however worthwhile – that solely confines them to their hotel. For by doing so, they miss out on excellent dining in and around the seaside resort.

As far as gourmet dining is concerned, Puerto Vallarta has a solid reputation, both in Mexico and abroad thanks in part to Chefs Thierry Blouet (Café des Artistes, see p 136) and Roger Dreier (Chez Roger, see p 135). What's more, countless young chefs have developed their art under the tutelage of one of these two pillars of Puerto Vallarta's gastronomical scene. Those trained by Thierry Blouet have been running away with prizes from national and international cooking competitions, one of these rising stars, Mexican chef Roberto Gómez, runs the show at Sazón.

This seaside city thus boasts a number of fine restaurants. Below you will find a selection of the best places in town, listed by area. Most restaurants are open seven days a week, for both lunch and dinner, during the high season. Lunch (*comida*) is usually served from 1pm on.

# THE OLD TOWN

## Isla Cuale and North of the Río Cuale

This is a city where upscale dining is common, and establishments offering authentic Mexican family fare are few and far between. There is, however, at least one exception: **La Corbeneta** *($-$$; Mon to Sat 2pm to 8pm, closed Sun; Calle Guerrero no. 123, one street south of the Malecón, near the ocean)*. Few tourists eat here and patrons are seated at communal tables with Mexican diners. There is no fixed menu, dishes change from day to day, and offerings range from beef pot-au-feu to simmered seafood. The prices are low, which is no doubt why this small, cramped establishment doesn't take credit cards.

The **Tangaroa** *($-$$$; daily noon to 10pm; Calle Perú no. 1308 at the corner of Nicaragua, & 2-68-98)* is our favourite restaurant, fancied by many Puerto Vallarta residents as well. It's run by a father and his sons. Offerings include *tostadas de mariscos* (spicy seafood served atop grilled *tortillas*), a fish fillet done to perfection, served with vegetables and an aromatic sauce, and a magnificent dish of crisp, tasty crayfish cooked in a fragrant *court-bouillon*.

Well-located on the first floor of a building on the Malecón, **La Chata** *($$-$$$; daily 11am to 11pm; Calle Paseo Díaz Ordaz no. 708, ☎3-16-84 or 3-16-85)* is a somewhat pretentious place that basically offers American fast-food and culinary curiosities that are unrelated to traditional Mexican dishes. Thus, the *sopa de arroz* is not, contrary to what you'd expect, a rice soup, but rather rice sautéed with ham and served on a tiny plate. Too chic for words! The house specialty is *pozole*, a concoction of corn, pimentos, herbs and meat. There's dancing to the sounds of guitars, *bandolinas*, tambourines and panpipes.

**La Dolce Vita** *($$-$$$; Thu to Sat noon to 2am Sun 6pm to 2am; Calle Paseo Díaz Ordaz no. 274, ☎2-38-52)* is another eatery set amidst the non-stop action of the trendy Malecón, the promenade along the ocean. It offers pastas or pizzas cooked in wood-burning ovens. From Thursday to Saturday, this restaurant vibrates to the sounds of jazz.

A little off the beaten path in the north part of town, **La Bamba** *($$$-$$$$$; 4pm to 11pm; Brasilia near Libramiento, ☎3-08-57)* occupies the top floor of a house in a residential district where tourists would not necessarily find themselves in otherwise. It is therefore best to get good directions while making your reservation. The house motto could very well be "We are better off here than below!" Indeed, the back terrace overlooks a cemetery. But this is not the only view offered here. All around sprawls a lively neighbourhood and, in the distance, the majestic Bahía de Banderas (Bay of Flags) in all its splendour, particularly at sunset. The Guerrero family jokingly claims that their *mariscos* (seafood) soup can rouse the dead! The place also serves good Mexican specialties such as guacamole, quesadillas, enchiladas, tacos, *chiles rellenos* (stuffed peppers) and *fajitas*. Another delicious treat: the fillet of fish served with the sauce of your choice, either *veracruzana*, garlic or *diabla* (very spicy). The lobster, shrimp, chicken and steak come either grilled whole or in brochettes. All dishes are properly seasoned. The food is good, but the bill is somewhat high for this kind of cuisine. There's some talk of the restaurant moving to Calle Basilio Badillo, south of the Río Cuale, to be closer to the bustling city. Check if the place has moved before heading out needlessly or, better yet, call first.

Somewhat removed from the action, the very popular **Pipis** *($$$; daily 1pm to 11pm; Calle Guadalupe Sánchez no. 804, at the corner of Calle de Pipila, ☎3-27-67)* prepares *pozole* in soup form (a consommé enriched with chicken pieces, corn, lettuce and onion), laced with lemon juice, pimento and fresh oregano. Other specialties include chilis *rellenos* (two green peppers stuffed with cheese, breaded, fried and served with a bean sauce), *fajitas*, *enchiladas poblanas* and delightful *margaritas*, which the establishment prepares according to a special house recipe.

**Ritos Baci** *($$$; daily 1pm to midnight; Calle Josefa Ortiz De Domínguez no. 181, ☎2-64-48)* is a small establishment that is not very well known in Puerto Vallarta, yet it serves good Italian cuisine and will even deliver meals to your hotel or studio apartment. All dishes are made from family recipes. On the menu: pizzas, pastas, hot or cold Italian sandwiches, chocolate cake, strawberry cake and ice cream.

At **Chez Roger** *($$$-$$$$$; Mon to Sat 6:30pm to 1am; closed Sun; Calle Augustin Rodríguez no. 267, ☎2-59-00),* Swiss chef-owner Roger Dreier's cuisine is both classic, innovative and creative. The merely hungry can enjoy simple pastas or Swiss fondues, while gourmets can savour splendid and unusual dishes. Dreier's most attractive, tastiest concoctions include red snapper with shrimp in lobster-flavoured hollandaise sauce, and grilled fish with puréed pimento and tequila. The restaurant serves excellent desserts, including a delectable hot chocolate ("bloc") and *fruta* (fruit on custard with strawberry sauce). The upstairs terrace overlooks a magnificent flower-filled courtyard. Staff speak English, French and German.

**Café Trio** *($$$-$$$$$; every day noon to 4pm and 6pm to 2am; Guerrero no. 264, ☎2-21-96)* stands out on account of its simplicity. In Puerto Vallarta's restaurant milieu, preparations are often an excuse to impress tourists. Such pretentions are out of place at Trio, where co-owners Peter Lodes and Bernhard Guth offer genuine, delicious and comforting cuisine. Indeed, you won't find any useless, pedantic culinary "fusions" here; moreover, the food is harmoniously seasoned. Located near the cathedral, this small restaurant resembles a French bistro, simply decorated with wooden chairs and tables as well as beautiful paintings adorning the walls. At lunch, you can sample such starters as *mesclun* with olive-oil dressing and tapenade or a salad made of local tomatoes (*jitomate*) and onions with basil dressing. And for the main course: lamb raviolis on a bed of fine ratatouille and aniseed-flavoured sorbet; escalope of wiener schnitzel and fries. All the (very healthy) freshly-squeezed juices are prepared at a moment's notice with seasonal fruits and vegetables, such as pineapple-celery-orange or banana-nut-pear. Dishes featured on the dinner menu are more elaborate. Latecomers can also feast on a good steak with salad and fries until 2am.

Vaguely evoking a Mexican country feel, **Rio Grande** *($$$-$$$$$; every day 8am to 11pm; Avenida México no. 1175, ☎2-00-95)* keeps with tradition without bringing any originality to its culinary offerings. Though locals seem to enjoy the food, tourists will be a little disappointed. Featured on the menu are empanadas (fried, shrimp-stuffed pastry turnovers sprinkled with lemon juice); *sopa de mariscos*, a hearty seafood (mostly octopus and shrimp) soup; the *sarandeado* fish – ours was lacking in freshness – normally barbecued (ours seemed fried!) and topped with chili sauce. The restaurant also makes a scrumptious caramel flan.

Impossible to miss, located on the Malecón, the ubiquitous **Planet Hollywood** *($$$-$$$$$; every day 11am to 2am; Morelo no. 518, ☎3-27-10)* features a mammoth Hollywood-style movie decor. Indeed, the place aims to dazzle... Walls plastered with posters of male and female actors who have delighted millions of American movie buffs, videos playing on a giant screen and even a souvenir shop. The menu features Italian-American cuisine and a smattering of regionally-inspired dishes, including the New Orleans-style blackened-chicken sandwich and shrimp, St. Louis ribs and Santa Fe chicken linguini, as well as Puerto Vallarta shrimp-and-crab *ceviche* and the (low-fat) turkey burger, all of which come with a generous helping of fries.

Located near the cathedral, **Abadía Bassó** *($$$$-$$$$$; Wed to Mon 5pm to midnight; Hidalgo no. 224, ☎2-13-74)* provides a thoroughly Mexican ambiance; the warm yet light decor is accentuated by orange-hued colours and enhanced with lovely handicrafts. The cuisine is Mediterranean, with a few French, Italian and Greek culinary influences. Items on the menu include home-made terrine, stuffed turkey, champagne-marinated oysters, beef Wellington and tiramisu.

At the **Café des Artistes** *($$$$ at noon and $$$$$ in the evening; Calle Guadalupe Sánchez no. 740, ☎2-32-28)*, the garden features gorgeous sculptures and fountains by Jesús Botello Sánchez, better known as "Tellosa". The interior walls are decorated with paintings and frescoes in a variety of styles. Chef Blouet, for his part, is a culinary artist, and gastronomy reaches new heights at his restaurant. Avocado crab with mango and cumin vinaigrette, cold melon bisque speckled with mint yogurt and shrimp ravioli with sun-dried tomatoes and champagne sauce are just a few of his ingenious creations. Peking duck, chicken with dates and prunes and red snapper with crab arrive at the table with exotic garnishes like pimento, ginger and cactus. His chocolate crème brûlée, almond biscuits and pistachio ice cream make for an exquisite end to the meal. English and French spoken.

Not overly modest and in a lovely setting where Mexican artists are found, **Le Bistro** *($$$$$; every day 9am to midnight; Isla Río Cuale no. 16A, ☎2-02-83)* offers diners a few creations by in-house chef Francisco Alvarez as well as classics that uphold its fine reputation despite the high prices. Featured on the menu are escargots with garlic-herb butter; Vallarta Crab Sashimi; smoked-salmon-and-pear salad; Coconut Tempura Shrimp Royale; "Chicken des Artistes" (tender rock Cornish hen stuffed with a blend of herbed rice, dried fruit and nuts served on fettucine topped with mango-cilantro sauce); Filet Mignon Bordeaux; steamed or grilled lobster with garlic butter; Ginger Ice Cream; and Mango Sour Cream Flan.

Another "Tellosa" sculpture stands in **La Cuiza** *($$$$$; Wed to Mon 5pm to 11pm, closed Tue; Isla Río Cuale no. 3, ☎2-56-46)*, a café-restaurant whose pretty terrace is surrounded by greenery. Jazz concerts *(Thu to Sun 8pm to 11pm)* add to the atmosphere and attract lots of fans. The menu consists of fruit-based dishes. The sweet and savoury flavours seem to appeal to some people. No doubt inspired by universal cuisine, the food artists here have given their appetizers and dishes such names as Cuiza Satay, Sun Pizza, St. Moritz Crab Cakes, Tuna Tamarindo and Calamari New Orleans. Also on the menu are Mexican-influenced dishes such as the Huachinango Majahuita (or Majahuita Red Snapper), coated with garlic and toasted sesame then pan grilled and served with papaya-mango-chili sauce, as well as more "traditional" dishes, including the filet mignon with red-wine sauce and mushrooms.

## South of the Río Cuale

Calle Basilio Badillo is known as the *calle de los cafés*. Indeed, on either side of this bustling thoroughfare are a succession of bars, cafés, restaurants and *taquerías*.

Until recently, the **Café Lido** *($-$$; 8am to 8pm; Calle Basilio Badillo no. 206, ☎2-23-79)* bore the appealing name

"Aux Deux Dauphins", but because that name already existed in Puerto Vallarta, the owner had to change it. Swiss-born Rita Krunz, the friendly, charming proprietress, has transformed the terrace and marvellous courtyard of her *hacienda* into a café. It's the perfect place to have a snack or drink under shady umbrellas, sampling tasty fruit drinks, including an absolutely delectable whipped banana yogurt. Light meals are available, including salads, hamburgers, sandwiches and cold cuts. Rita makes most of the cakes, and her espresso is among the best in Puerto Vallarta. Note that she plans to add a restaurant to her house soon. The new establishment will offer a wide range of *tapas*, the bite-sized tidbits served in Spain as appetizers with drinks. In addition to the classic Spanish varieties, *tapas* will come in assorted international flavours: Thai, French, Italian, Chinese, Vietnamese and, of course, Swiss and Mexican. Besides German, her mother tongue, Rita speaks perfect English, French and Spanish.

The top floor of the **Andale** nightclub *($-$$$; every day 24 hours; Olas Altas no. 425, ☎2-10-54 or 3-06-84)* has been converted into a restaurant. Hearty American-style breakfasts as well as burgers, ribs, shrimp and osso bucco milanaise are served here at any time of day or night.

**La Casa de Los Hot Cakes - The Pancake House** *($$; every day 8am to 2pm; Calle Basilio Badillo no. 289, ☎2-62-72)* is a single establishment that bears two names. Late risers and aficionados of American breakfasts can stuff themselves here on fruit pancakes smothered in Log Cabin Syrup, rubbery omelets, eggs Benedict with packaged sauce, muffins, chocolate crepes topped with whipped cream and lots of other hearty dishes, all served in a pretty garden full of mangoes and bananas. American tourists love this place because to them, it's gourmet heaven, so you may have to wait at the bar until a table is free.

The **Balam** *($$-$$$; noon to midnight; Calle Basilio Badillo no. 425, ☎2-34-51)*, decorated entirely by local artists, is popular among Puerto Vallarta residents and fans of fresh seafood. Fishermen supply the restaurant with their daily catch of fish and seafood, which is then grilled or simmered in a variety of delicious ways. Specialties worth sampling include shrimp *empanadas*, seafood salad, oyster soup, *ceviche*, red snapper with almonds, grilled rock lobster, seafood spaghetti, coffee-liqueur pie and flambéed bananas.

🦞 At the **Café de Olla** *($$-$$$; Wed to Mon noon to 11pm, closed Tue; Calle Basilio Badillo no. 168, ☎3-16-26)*, owners Juan Sosa and Hildebia Avalos offer excellent family fare, and all their dishes are authentically Mexican. They specialize in grilled meat, fish and seafood. The place is packed with tourists every night. The service is so speedy that as you're eating your soup, you're watching you main dish get cold — soup and main courses are served at the same time! The *margaritas* served in this establishment are absolutely enormous. The room is dark and stuffy, even though it has many fans. Throughout the meal, a parade of *mariachis* keep diners entertained.

Club Meza del Mar's restaurant, **Alejandro's** *($$-$$$; every day noon to 2pm and 6pm to 9pm; Amapas, no. 380, ☎2-48-88)*, stands on a terrace, overlooks the sea and offers a buffet for guests who have opted for the hotel's all-inclusive package. The menu features seafood dishes and Mexican specialties. A band performs here three times a week.

A charming terrace painted in the white and blue colours of Greece heralds the **Karpathos Taverna** *($$-$$$$; Mon to Sat 9am to 11pm; Rodolfo Gómez, no. 110)*, but only early birds get to sit near the street. Thus, it may be best to take advantage of the air-conditioned interior, arranged in typical Greek-*psarotaverna* style. The restaurant offers patrons the classics of Hellenic cuisine: tzaziki, taramasalata, roasted lamb, moussaka, baklava and much more.

🦞 Swiss-born Heinz Reize speaks English, French and Spanish with as much ease as German, his native tongue. After having spent many years in Montreal and as manager of the Kristal Vallarta hotel, Reize has recently set up the **Coco Tropical - Restaurant Grill & Beach Club** *($$-$$$$; every day noon to 1am; Basilio Badillo no. 246, ☎2-54-85)* on a lovely terrace. On the golden sands of Playa Olas Altas, this little paradise is just the place for those who wish to sink their teeth into a good 200 or 500 gram New York or Cowboy steak. The grilled chicken is also eaten with relish; it is so delicious! The tomato-based Azteca soup served with tortillas, cream and mild cheese as well as the shrimp tamales are also a must, as are the excellent apple pie and creamy chocolate mousse.

**Daiquiri Dick's** *($$-$$$$$; every day 9am to 11pm; Olas Altas no. 314, ☎2-05-66)* consists of a roofed terrace located on Playa Los Muertos. The chef is Mexican, but ventures into "California Grill" cuisine. Among the dishes to be sampled here are the meal-sized pesto grilled-chicken salad; traditional Mexican black-bean soup; grilled tuna steak with cilantro-chili sauce; fillet of fish with fruit sauce; and breast of chicken with bacon, cheese and curry-mushroom sauce.

A large *palapa* structure stands out from the others as much for its architecture as its style, which, when espied from the approaches to Playa Olas Altas, looks fairly obtrusive. Indeed, **Nanahuatzin** *($$-$$$$$; every day 8am to 11pm; Olas Altas no. 336, ☎2-05-77 or 2-49-77)* has a terrace whose decor is somewhat more ornate than that of its counterparts. The menu features dishes that will satisfy Mexican and North American tastes alike: Caesar salad, Fisherman's Tribute (fillet of fish stuffed with fresh shellfish baked in a tomato-wine sauce and topped with melted cheese); *mole poblano*; and caramel crepes.

**La Palapa** *($$$; every day 8am to 11pm; Calle Amapas no. 124; Playa Los Muertos, near Calle Púlpito, ☎2-52-25)* boasts an attractive outdoor dining area on Playa Los Muertos with a panoramic view over the Bahía des Banderas. It offers excellent Mexican cuisine as well as reliable grilled meat and fish dishes. See also "A Gourmet Tour of Puerto Vallarta", p 32. Ideally located, the restaurant is a favourite among beach-goers, who can dig into a big club sandwich or *hamburguesa* (hamburger) here.

The **Café Maximilien** *($$$; Mon to Sat 4 pm to 11pm, closed Sun; Calle Olas Altas no. 380-B, ☎3-07-60)* has exquisite food but the setup, with a few tables too close to the crowded sidewalk on calle Olas Altas, leaves something to be desired. The proprietor is Austrian, as was the Emperor Maximilian, but the chef is German. It therefore comes as no surprise that they serve schnitzels, sauerbraten wieners and apple strudel. The menu also features some "modern Mexican cuisine". Still, the European influence is obvious. Instead of *tortillas* in your soup, nicely spiced with grilled garlic and fresh herbs, you get bread. The food is delicious. The chicken breast (with bones and skin) served with rosemary on puréed pota- toes, roasted vegetables and mustard sauce, is aesthetically pleasing. Other specialties include grilled fish, lamb and beef.

Before Basilio Badillo, also known as "Calle de los Cafes", **Jalapeño's** *($$$-$$$$; 5pm to 11pm; Calle Basilio Badillo, no. 211)* specializes in charbroiled dishes. The owner is American, the cooks are Mexican and together they turn out good grilled fish, chicken and beef. The *tortilla* and the black- bean soups are excellent.

The Argentinian restaurant **Los Pibes** *($$$-$$$$$; every day noon to 11pm; Basilio Badillo no. 261, ☎3-15-57)* is easily recognizable by its enormous grill, which takes up almost the whole front area. It is the hallmark of the restaurant, which specializes in prime grilled meats.

Jean-Pierre LeBousicalt has taken it into his head to prepare the favourite dishes of American reporters at his aptly named **The Reporter Restaurant** *($$$-$$$$$; every day 9am to 11pm, Apr to Oct 5pm to 11pm; Ignacio L. Vallarta no. 230, ☎3-27-80)*. As such, the "Dan Rather" appetizer is a fish-and-seafood salad, the "Ed Bradley" dish an orange-glazed fillet of *mahi mahi*, the "Richard Kapplan" Bourbon ribs... well, you get the idea. The rest of the menu follows suit, offering a long list of such selections.

🦐 The Montreal Insectarium is not alone in offering adventur- ous gourmets the opportunity to savour insect ("bug") bro- chettes. **Los Laureles** *($$$-$$$$$; every day 2pm to midnight; Basilio Badillo no. 286, ☎2-02-56)* peppers its otherwise-typical Mexican menu with a few dishes as unusual as they are original, made of *chapulines* (grilled grasshoppers), *huazontles* (aromatic plants), *huitlacoches* (Mexican corn fungi), *escamoles* (ant eggs, Mexican caviar!) and *gusanos de maguey* (cactus worms). But more timid souls need not give a wide berth to the restaurant as it also offers excellent black-bean soup; *caldo loco* (crazy broth), traditional soup made with chicken, onions, rice and cheese; delicious lime soup (chicken consommé enhanced with lime juice, chicken and cheese); and last but not least, delectable dishes such as the breast of chicken prepared with three *moles* (one green with *chile poblano*, one red and

RESTAURANTS

another with *frijoles* (beans) and cheese). The fillet of fish with garlic and the *arrachera* (thinly sliced beef in sauce with guacamole, *frijoles* and onion) are equally delicious and not to be missed. Among the successful desserts, the rice pudding (*arroz con leche*) and the flan are two mouth-watering treats.

At the far end of the patio, **Café Frankfurt** *($$$-$$$$$; every day noon to 11:30pm; Basilio Badillo no. 300, ☎2-34-03)* offers patrons German beers, schnitzels and bratwursts as well as other Teutonic specialties, including the famous sauerkraut with meat.

**Archie's Wok** *($$$$; Calle Francisca Rodríguez, no. 130, ☎20-411)* is named after Filipino-American Archie Alpenia, who was film director John Huston's cook. Since Archie's death several years back, and despite attempts by his wife Cindy to keep standards up to par, this restaurant isn't what it once was. The setting is magnificent, but some dishes are truly disappointing. Avoid at all costs the sweet-and-sour dishes, which are prepared for American tastes and are too syrupy for true aficionados of Asian cuisine. Having said that, the spring rolls, the chicken with cashews and snow peas in oyster sauce and the garlic shrimp with ginger and coriander are good choices for those who like this kind of food. The proprietor speaks English and Spanish.

In a setting worthy of the French colonial era, but in a decor of vibrant Mexican colours, Frenchmen Marc Bernard and Philippe Maurice, the chef, opened the **Café Olé** *($$$$$; every day 5pm to 11pm; Calle Basilio Badillo no. 283, ☎2-28-77)* after several years' apprenticeship in China, Thailand and Japan. In addition to the freshest Mexican produce, the chef favours fine imported foodstuffs: New Zealand venison, Australian lamb, Nova Scotia salmon and Mediterranean mussels are all on the menu. You can eat on the terrace area overlooking the street or in the air-conditioned dining room. Avoid the flashy dishes prepared at your table, which have little flavour.

The outdoor dining areas at **El Palomar de los Gonzáles** *($$$$$; every day 6pm to 11pm; Calle Aguacate no. 425, ☎2-07-95)* overlook the city of Puerto Vallarta, providing front-row seats for the spectacular *puesta del sol* (sunset), when the bay, the harbour and the surrounding mountains are bathed in brilliant reds and pinks. It's a great place for a before-dinner drink, but steer clear of its dishes which lack in taste and are quite expensive. This restaurant is a tourist trap; you're better off going back down around Basilio Badillo.

 **Adobe Café** *($$$$$; every day 6pm to 11pm; Basilio Badillo no. 252, ☎2-67-20)* upholds its gourmet thoroughfare's excellent reputation. The decor is spectacularly reminiscent of adobes, traditional houses constructed of sun-dried clay bricks. Chef Vincente Montes revives traditional cuisine with new ingredients combined in an innovative way to give his dishes a light and fresh quality. Featured on the menu are fresh lettuce leaves with feta cheese; sweet chili-glazed chicken wings; cream of cilantro with clams; tortilla soup; fillet of *huachinango* with mango-flavoured hollandaise sauce; jumbo coconut-coated grilled shrimp served with apple sauce; tenderloin of beef stuffed with *huitlacoches* (Mexican corn fungi) and served in cheese sauce; coffee flan and coconut-mango cheesecake.

People come to **Sr. Chico's** *($$$$$; every day 5:30pm to 11:30pm; Púlpito no. 373, ☎2-35-70)* for the view it offers of Puerto Vallarta and its surroundings. The cuisine itself, however, is not very exciting. Certain dishes are prepared by the server at your table, including the Baja Shrimp with bacon, mushrooms, spinach and a white-wine sauce; the "Three Friends": filet mignon, lobster and shrimp; and the bananas flambée.

## ✖ SOUTHERN PUERTO VALLARTA

Innumerable restaurants vie for attention along the Mismaloya beach. On the south shore of the Río Mismaloya, their outdoor dining areas are jammed together on the sand, which you inevitably have to walk on to get from one place to the next. Along the way, each restaurant shows off its menu and tries to attract patrons. The **Ramada Miramar** *($-$$; every day 9am to 6pm; Mismaloya beach)*, in the middle of the beach, is a good place to stop for a snack. It offers shrimp and fish *empanadas*, *quesadillas*, shrimp brochettes and fillet of *huachinango*. The French fries are excellent and the service is appealingly casual.

RESTAURANTS

Note that this establishment does not take credit cards. Also be sure to ask for your change!

At the **Blue Bay Club, El Embarcadero**, *($$-$$$; every day 7am to 10:30am, 1pm to 3pm and 7pm to 10pm; Carretera a Barra de Navidad, Km 4, ☎1-55-00)* lays out buffets for hotel guests and members of its beach club. Served here is so-called international cuisine, with a choice of several ready-made dishes as well as pastas, salads and a tempting dessert counter. The place also offers guests a lovely view of the bay. Also on site is **La Hacienda** *($$-$$$$$; every day 6:30am to 10:30pm)*, which offers Mexican specialties, and **The Grill House** *($$$$$; 6:30pm to 10pm)*, which prepares all kinds of grilled meats: ribs, chicken, steak, etc.

The **La Noche de la Iguana** *($$-$$$$; every day 10am to 11pm; km 12.5, Carretera a Barra de Navidad, Mismaloya)*, as its name suggests, is located above the famous location where *Night of the Iguana* was shot. You can still see traces of the Hollywood film below the steep steps at the end of the promenade that leads to the Mismaloya beach; it's much easier to get to this restaurant by the road. The outdoor dining area on the sand overlooks the bay. A typical meal here might consist of salad, turtle soup, a plate of shrimp and dessert, for $16 US *(no credit cards)*.

**Chico's Paraíso** *($$-$$$; every day 1am to 7pm; km 20 Carretera a Barra de Navidad, ☎2-07-47)* is one of many eateries standing at a bend in the Río Los Horcones, where a torrent of water cuts through the rocks. The restaurant was built from stone and its collection of *palapas* is designed to blend in with the natural surroundings. The menu features mainly fish and seafood, but also *quesadillas*, a tasty *guacamole* and a sinful coconut pie *(no credit cards)*. It costs 82 pesos to get here by taxi from downtown Puerto Vallarta, 24 pesos from Boca de Tomaltán.

**Chino's Paraíso** *($$$-$$$$$; every day 10am to 5pm; Río Mismaloya Charco Azul Riviera Norte, ☎5-04-79)*, lies across from the Mismaloya beach, 2 km along a winding road that forks to the left after the village. Sheltered by palm trees, the building was designed to harmonize with the environment. Located in the forest near waterfalls, Chino's is known for its grilled seafood, frog's legs, fish fillet and grilled chicken. Some say the prices are a bit high, however.

The **Kliff** *($$$-$$$$$; every day noon to 10:30pm; km 17.5 Carretera a Barra de Navidad, Mismaloya, ☎89-06-66 or 4-09-75)*, perched atop a cliff, is the biggest *palapas* building in the Americas. The restaurant is laid out on several open-air platforms beneath large, circular roofs made of palm leaves (*palapas*), and can seat 600 patrons. The food, however, fails to match the impressive setting. The selection is rather limited, offering American and Mexican dishes like crabmeat avocado soup, Louisiana gumbo, a "surf 'n' turf" platter, fish and seafood dishes, spaghetti, etc.

Further along the road, before Boca de Tomaltlán, the enormous **Che Che** *($$$-$$$$$; Mon to Sat 10am to 5pm, closed Sun; km 17, Carretera a Barra de Navidad, Boca de Tomaltlán, ☎4-01-08)* serves traditional dishes you don't usually find in Puerto Vallarta restaurants. They include steam-cooked chicken in a banana leaf, marinated octopus, pork hock "*achiote*" and several seafood-based dishes. The *tortillas* are made on the premises. You can reach the restaurant by going down a long trail to the seaside. The return trip, obviously, is harder.

The major tourist resort that is **La Jolla de Mismaloya** *($$$$$; every day 8am to 11:30pm; Mismaloya, on the hill to the right, just before the village, ☎8-06-60)* houses two restaurants worth a few visits. **La Iguana Italiana** *($$$-$$$$$; everyday 6pm to 1am; Playa Mismaloya, ☎8-06-60)* boasts an elegant setting dominated by attractive woodwork. Moreover, the cuisine here is much appreciated by lovers of Italian food. Selections from the menu include fettucine Alfredo; seafood cannelloni; white-wine-glazed escalopes of veal served with risotto; and salmon-and-goat-cheese pizza. The restaurant also has a lounge reserved for cigar lovers; the bar offers over 100 different brands of tequila.

At the same hotel, **El Patio Steak House** *($$$-$$$$$; every day 8am to 11pm)* overlooks the beach. As its name suggests, this restaurant offers steak as well as an excellent rib of beef. All the meat dishes here are tasty and delightfully juicy.

The Camino Real on the Playa Las Estacas is home to **La Perla** *($$$$$; every day 7pm to midnight; Camino Real Hotel, Playa Las Estacas, ☎1-50-00)*, which serves up excellent French and Mexican cuisine. The menu offers many inviting and unique dishes, like cactus salad with crisp greenery, mussel soup au gratin with coconut, rack of lamb with peanuts and amaranth flowers, duck breast glazed with guava honey, grilled fillet of *huachinango* (red snapper) with Mexican mushrooms in Poblano pepper sauce, and coconut shrimp in mango sauce.

On the rock-dotted beach, the **El Set** bar-restaurant *($$$$$; Carretera a Barra de Navidad, Km 2.5, ☎1-53-42 or 1-53-41)* is partially shaded by a huge hevea and braided palm trellisses. Its lovely terrace looking out on the Pacific Ocean has no doubt contributed to its popularity. The mainly North American clientele here enjoys Mexican-flavoured dishes such as the *fajita* combo of beef, chicken and pork with Indian sauce au gratin. Also on the menu are seafood with garlic butter as well as crêpes suzettes for dessert.

# ✕ THE NORTHERN HOTEL ZONE

 **La Guacamaya** *($$$-$$$$; every day 7am to 11pm; Francisco Medina Ascencio, Km 3.5, ☎6-17-00)*, the Holiday Inn's poolside restaurant, provides a generous buffet featuring a good choice of ready-cooked dishes (about fifteen), seafood, meats and vegetables. The dishes are simple, but made with quality ingredients. A few examples: tomato-potato soup; cabbage soup; watercress-and-mushroom salad; green vegetables (beans, broccoli, christophines); mashed yams; roast pork *en jus*; spaghetti with meat sauce; seafood (clams, crab, scallops, etc.) in sauce; pound cake with syrup; crème caramel (turned out of its mould); etc. Patrons — several of whom are not guests of the hotel — line up for the hearty burgers made with a good-sized barbecued beef patty and dressed with the garnishes of your choice.

French and Italian cuisine are both available at **Avanzaré** *($$$$$; Mon to Sat 6pm to midnight; Francisco Medina Ascencio, Km 3.5, Holiday Inn, ☎6-17-00)*. Guests can opt for one or the other, for the two are never combined, as is unfortunately all-too often the case. Amidst a heterogeneous decor graced with a grand piano, patrons here sit on small, low-backed stools or well-padded colonial-style seats to savour such treats as the "concert" of tuna, beef and shrimp carpaccio or salmon-and-tuna tartare, and even country-style pesto soup. These are then followed by Pernod-flambéed butterfly shrimp, herb-coated fillet of bass or the rack of lamb with garlic sauce.

The **Sheration Buganvilias** hotel houses four restaurants, distributed throughout the main floors of its eight towers. One of them, the **Café Bistro Las Gaviotas** *($$$$$; every day 6pm to midnight; Sheraton Buganvilias, Francisco Medina Ascencio no. 999, ☎3-04-04)*, offers international cuisine essentially consisting of steaks and seafood, as well as a bountiful salad bar and live music every night. Another, **El Mirador** *($$$$$; every day 5pm to 11pm; ☎3-04-04)*, set on a lovely *palapa*-covered terrace, specializes in Italian food. A third and more casual option is **La Villita** *($$$-$$$$; every day 5pm to 11pm)*, which serves delicious sandwiches and various Mexican offerings. Last but not least comes **El Chiringuito** *($$-$$$; every day noon to 5pm)*, a simple snack bar.

 The **Fiesta Americana** hotel boasts an excellent Mexican restaurant, **La Hacienda** *($$$$$; every day 6pm to midnight; Fiesta Americana hotel, ☎4-20-10)* which serves tasteful and innovatively prepared dishes in a rustic, colonial-style setting. Featured on the menu are shrimp and *nopalitos* (cactus); cream of Roquefort cheese; shrimp-stuffed fillet of fish with corn sauce; lobster enchiladas with cheese and *salsa verde*; and corn bread.

# ✕ MARINA VALLARTA

On the Marina piers, restaurants squashed between shops of all sorts struggle to give their outdoor dining areas at least a modicum of ambiance. Despite their efforts, there is little warmth to these places. Still, **Mr. Nopal** *($$-$$$; every day 8am to 11pm; Marina Vallarta, ☎1-02-72, ext. 2007)* stands out among this unappealing group of establishments. Located within an enclosure of low gray brick walls, the restaurant has a Mexican decor lit up by a medley of bright colours. In this otherwise modern and resolutely bourgeois area, it makes for a welcome contrast. The Mexican proprietor offers several

RESTAURANTS

interesting specialties, including an avocado stuffed with *huitlacoche* (a local mushroom), *caldo de haba con nopal y chile passilla* (bean soup with cactus and chilis) and *Mr. Nopal's camarones* (*nopal* means a large leaf or slab of cactus) garnished with cheese and a jumbo shrimp. What's more, the prices are reasonable.

Next door, the Italian restaurant **La Terraza** *($$-$$$; every day 8am to midnight; Marina Vallarta, ☎1-05-60 or 1-02-62, ext. 1220)* has a modern decor and offers *arrabiata*, alfredo and *vongole* pasta dishes, as well as raviolis, scampi and fish fillets. You can also dig into pizza fresh out of the oven.

The last restaurant along this Marina promenade, **Porto Bello** *($$$-$$$$$; every day noon to 11pm; Marina Vallarta, ☎1-00-03)* is run by a Torontonian and a Portuguese, the waiters and the menu are Italian and the food is thoroughly traditional. It has the usual *antipasti*, pastas, pizzas and veal and seafood dishes. Rest assured that the cuisine is excellent here. The pizza has a light, flaky crust and the perfectly cooked pasta dishes are prepared with fine ingredients and seasonings. If your stomach's in need of a rest, this place is a safe bet.

**Garibaldi's** *($$$-$$$$$; every day 1pm to 5pm and 6pm to midnight; Westin Regina Hotel, ☎1-03-22 or 3-28-00)* offers a wide selection of fish and seafood and a fishing-port ambiance to match. Suggestions by chef Antonio García include: the shrimp taco with Caesar salad, the *sarandeado* (barbecued) red snapper and the seafood risotto.

The Marriott CasaMagna hotel's restaurant, **Mikado** *($$$$$; every day 6pm to 11pm; Paseo de la Marina no. 5, Marriott CasaMagna, ☎1-00-04)* offers typical Japanese cuisine. Sushi, sashimi and various other specialties are prepared here with traditional ceremony by a chef armed with a dizzying array of knives. Stationed behind the grill, this samurai wields his knives in breathtaking fashion, to the great delight of American spectators who get a real kick out of seeing such prowess with the razor-sharp blades. Besides the classic miso soup, patrons here enjoy good vegetable and shrimp tempuras, satay or teriyaki chicken and beef, herb-sautéed fillet of fish perfectly matched with ginger vegetables and fried ice cream with chocolate sauce.

At the **Sazón** *($$$$; every day 6pm to midnight; 2nd floor, Las Iguanas shopping centre, Planta Alta, Marina Vallarta, ☎1-06-81 or 1-06-91)*, a restaurant-disco near Marina Vallarta, the wonderful Mexican chef, Roberto Gómez, and partner Thierry Blouet have concocted a fabulous menu. It offers appealing and extraordinary dishes like minced octopus with mushrooms and spicy pineapple sauce in a banana leaf; beef tongue with avocado, garlic and coriander; grilled fillet of sea bream with coriander; coffee-liqueur cheesecake and pumpkin caramel crepe.

Looking out on the Malecón and the piers of the marina, **Rincón de Buenos Aires** *($$$$$; every day 1pm to 11pm; Royal Pacific no. 127, ☎1-22-60)*, owned by the Argentinian-born Sánchez family, is renowned for its various cuts of barbecued beef. In addition to grilled meats, the menu features empanadas; seafood St-Jacques; Buenos Aires chicken supreme with ham, cheese and spinach; sweet-and-sour pork with tropical fruit; and fillet of *huachinango* with Roquefort.

The Velas Vallarta hotel's elegant restaurant, **Andrea** *($$$$$; every day 7:30am to 11pm; Avenida Costera no. 585, ☎1-00-91)* offers the refinements of Italian cuisine: shellfish au gratin, shrimp and calamari risotto; tomato-basil-bacon rigatoni; *picante* veal *scaloppina*; and tiramisu. An accordion player sometimes serenades diners, as well.

 NUEVO VALLARTA

**Club Marival Vallarta** has four restaurants. **Casa Bella** *($$-$$$; every day noon to 4pm and 6:30pm to 11pm; Bulevar Nuevo Vallarta, at Paseo de los Cocoteros S/N, ☎329-7-01-00)* puts out a varied lunch and dinner buffet, with magnificent ornamental cakes in the middle. At lunch, **Terraza Portofino** *($-$$$; every day 11am to 5pm and 6pm to 11pm)* is perfect for bathers and vacationers to have a quick bite to eat in an informal setting. Dinner is served on the terrace; the fixed-price menu offers four choices of dishes, including steak, grilled chicken and fish. The two other restaurants offer an *à-la-carte* menu: **La Pergola** *($-$$$; every day 7am to 11pm)* serves international cuisine, while **Bella Vista** *($$-$$$$; every day*

*6pm to 10pm)* serves Italian specialties in a more refined setting.

## AROUND PUERTO VALLARTA

---

## North

---

An authentic Mexican ambiance permeates **El Asadero** *($; every day 1pm to 7 pm; Calle 16 de Septiembre, Caminó al Rastro, Pitillal, ☎4-68-48)*, located in the suburbs and patronized mainly by locals. For a very reasonable price, you can dig into an all-you-can-eat dish of *carne asada*, a grilled, thinly sliced rib steak served with *guacamole*, fried onions and red beans. The corn *tortillas* are made on the premises and used in delicious *quesadillas* or *birrias* (stuffed with beef or chicken and swimming in a fiery hot sauce) or made into *jocoquis* (grilled *tortillas* with cheese). Charbroiled *chorizo* is another very popular house specialty.

While in Sayulita, be sure to check out **Don Pedro's** *($-$$$; Wed to Mon 8am to 10pm; Calle Marlin no. 02, ☎329-5-12-29)*, whose two tiered terraces overhang the beautiful beach. Served on the main-floor terrace are fast-food dishes such as burgers; club sandwiches; grilled chicken; crispy thin-crust pizza either with *chorizo*, onions, *chile poblano*, black beans and cilantro or with shrimp, garlic, bacon, tomato, basil and cheese. Upstairs, chef and co-owner Nicólas Parrillo puts his years of training in Los Angeles, California to the test with his tuna carpaccio, pesto minestrone and seafood pasta, moussaka, home-smoked marlin salad and his oven-roasted breast of duck glazed with balsamic vinegar and honey. The restaurant also makes a very good espresso.

**Miramar** *($$; every day noon to 7pm; Manzanilla beach, Cruz de Huanacastle)* offers fabulously fresh fish and seafood. It preserves its excellent reputation and defends its title as the best place for fresh seafood. The small outdoor dining area, sheltered by a roof of woven palm leaves, attracts many local artists who come to enjoy deliciously prepared mussels, giant scallops, conches, rock lobster, crabs and *huachinango* (red snapper).

*Pescado sarandeado* is a smoked fish grilled on wood charcoal in a traditional way that's still popular in the region today. The dish is a trademark at both the **Acuario** and **El Anclote** restaurants *($$$; every day 8am to 8pm; El Anclote beach)*. Their menus are similar, offering seafood soup, grilled rock lobster and fish fillets, along with more basic meals like *hamburguesas* (hamburgers), *fajitas* and grilled chicken.

## South

In the heart of the village of El Tuito, opposite the bus stop, is the **Nuevo Restaurant Nena** *($; every day 7:30am to 9pm; ☎322-8-00-93)*, the best place in town for a refreshing drink. Despite its lack of cleanliness, owner María Magdalena prepares good home-style cooking: beef and chicken soup *(caldo de rez, caldo de pollo)*; grilled beef or pork with sauce *(carne de rez en salsa roja, puerco en salsa verde)*. Lighter meals are also offered such as *quesadillas* (cheese-stuffed tortillas) and *dorados* tacos, rolled and stuffed with cheese and cream. The tortillas are prepared in a traditional oven on request.

RESTAURANTS

 MENU GLOSSARY

| | |
|---|---|
| aperitif | *aperitivo* |
| beef | *vaca* |
| beer | *cerveza* |
| bill | *la cuenta* |
| breakfast | *desayuno* |
| brochette | *brocheta* |
| butter | *mantequilla* |
| canapé | *tapas* |
| capsicum (pepper) | *pimiento* |
| chicken | *pollo* |
| clam | *almeja* |
| coffee | *café* |
| crayfish | *langosta* |
| credit card | *tarjeta de crédito* |
| cup or mug | *taza* |
| cutlet | *chuleta* |
| dessert | *postre* |
| dinner (or supper) | *cena* |

| | |
|---|---|
| to drink | *beber* |
| a drink | *bebida* |
| eat | *comer* |
| fish | *pescado* |
| fork | *tenedor* |
| French fries | *papas fritas* |
| fruit | *fruta* |
| fruit juice | *jugo de fruta* |
| glass | *vaso* |
| grilled food | *parrilla* |
| hamburger | *hamburguesa* |
| hors-d'oeuvre (or appetizer) | *entremese* |
| hot dog | *perro caliente* |
| ice cream | *helado* |
| ice cube | *hielo* |
| infusion (tea) | *infusión* |
| knife | *cuchillo* |
| ladies' room | *crevicios para damas* |
| lemon | *limón* |
| lobster | *bogavante or cangrejo* |
| lunch | *comida* |
| meal | *comida* |
| meat | *carne* |
| men's room | *crevicios para caballeros* |
| menu | *menú* |
| milk | *leche* |
| mussel | *mejillón* |
| napkin | *servilleta* |
| oil | *aceite* |
| plate | *plato* |
| pepper | *pimienta* |
| portion of | *una orden de* |
| receipt | *recibido* |
| red snapper | *huachinango* |
| reservation | *reserva* |
| restaurant | *restaurante* |
| rice | *arroz* |
| salt | *sal* |
| sauce | *salsa* |
| scallop | *pechina* |
| scampi | *langosta* |
| seafood | *mariscos* |
| shrimp | *camarón* |
| snack bar | *potana or antojito* |

| soup | *sopa* |
| spicy sauce | *salsa picante* |
| spoon | *cuchara* |
| straw | *paja* |
| sugar | *azúcar* |
| swordfish | *espadón montante* |
| table | *mesa* |
| tablecloth | *mantel* |
| tea | *té* |
| terrace | *terraza* |
| tip | *propina* |
| travellers' cheque | *cheque de viaje or viajero* |
| tuna | *atún* |
| turkey | *pava* |
| veal | *ternero* |
| vegetable | *verdura* |
| vinegar | *vinagre* |
| water | *agua* |
| distilled water | *agua destilada* |
| sparkling water | *agua guaseosa* |
| mineral water | *agua minerale* |
| red wine | *vino tinto* |
| white wine | *vino blanco* |

**RESTAURANTS**

## Helpful Phrases in Restaurants

| Waiter! | Mesero! or Joven! |
| May I please see the menu? | ¿Por favor, puedo ver el menú? |
| I'm hungry | Tengo hambre |
| What do you have to eat/drink? | ¿Qué hay de comer/tomar? |
| What do you recommend? | ¿Qué me aconseja? |
| I'd like a little more... | Quisiera mas... |
| Where are the washrooms? | ¿Donde estan los servicios? |
| I'd like the bill, please | Quisiera la cuenta, por favor |
| Thank you very much! | Muchas gracias! |

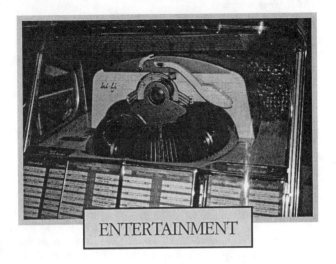

## ENTERTAINMENT

**P**uerto Vallarta is crammed with night spots that offer a whole range of diversions: lavish shows, folk groups contemporary bands, jazz concerts, disco music, etc. In the bars and cafés along the Malecón, the seaside promenade, night-owls can always find somewhere to dance to the rhythm of their favourite music. And come the end of the night, you can grab a late-night snack at most of these establishments because they are also restaurants.

 THE OLD TOWN

### North of the Río Cuale

**Stars Vallarta** *(2pm to 3am; Calle Zaragoza no. 160, south side of Plaza de Armas, ☎2-20-61 or 2-60-62)* caters to pool players. It's six tables are on the third floor, from where players can enjoy a good view of the Malecón and Puerto Vallarta's magnificent cathedral, whose steeple is topped with a crown. The lower floors house a restaurant and a bar-nightclub.

The **Hard Rock Café** *(Paseo Díaz Ordaz no. 652, ☎2-55-32)* is, of course, the place to go for rock music. Both lively and noisy, so it is a good bet for visitors who want to let off some steam. Bands play here from 11pm to 2am.

A young crowd dances to techno, house, reggae and disco beats at the **Zoo** club *(every day 24 hours; Paseo Díaz Ordaz no. 630, ☎2-49-45)*, located on the Malecón. The club's dancefloor is perhaps the busiest and wildest in town – a real zoo indeed.

At the **Carlos O'Brians** bar-restaurant *(Paseo Díaz Ordaz no. 786, ☎2-14-44)*, patrons tend to drink rather than eat. It is a favourite *gringo* watering-hole. Its Irish ambiance and American-style service is to some people's taste... and it's certainly lively. Visitors looking for this kind of thing should check out the action here.

Jazz, blues and some modern music are on tap at the quiet **Bar Deco** *(6pm to 2am; Calle Morelos no. 779, 6pm to 2am, ☎2-01-80)*. Small bands play here every night.

**El Panorama** *(6pm to 3am; 9th floor of La Siesta hotel; Calle Josefa Ortiz Domínguez y Miramar, behind the cathedral, ☎2-18-18)* is a bar-restaurant perched on a hill that boasts a panoramic view over Puerto Vallarta and its harbour. A nice place for an aperitif or, later in the evening, a drink while listening to one of the excellent bands.

Buzzed by *tequila*, tourists party until the small hours of the morning at the popular **Mr. Tequila's Grill** *(Calle Galeana no. 101-104, ☎2-57-25 or 2-27-33)*.

## South of the Río Cuale

At the cabaret-style **Mariachi Loco** *(nightly; Calle Lazaro Cárdenas no. 254, at the corner of Ignacio L. Vallarta, ☎3-22-05)*, patrons dine at tables decked out with Mexican colours. The establishment has a *taquería*, a counter that serves up plentiful tacos, burritos and other typical dishes. But locals and tourists come here mainly to hear the *mariachi* bands. A master of ceremonies who is also a singer (Victor Andrade the night we were there) takes to the large stage to entertain the crowd in Spanish; such places are relatively rare, and this one is invariably filled with an appreciative audience.

The rhythm-and-blues at the **Roxy** *(open nightly; Calle Ignacio L. Vallarta, at the corner of Francisco I. Madero)* is provided by various bands from the United States and Canada. A few lonely Americans sit around the low tables. During happy hour *(8pm to 10pm)* the place is packed with noisy fun-seekers.

The **Andales** bar-restaurant *(noon to 2am; Calle Olas Altas no. 425, ☎2-10-54)* is patronized by Puerto Vallarta residents who dance until dawn to the Mexican music.

The **Cactus** *(Wed to Sat; at the corner of Calle Constitución and Manuel M. Diéguez)* is one of the most popular discotheques in town. All customers are body searched at the door. Seats are arranged in tiers around the room and facing the dance floor. This bar is only open at night.

**La Iguana - Fiesta Mexicana** *(Thu and Sun, 7pm to 11pm; Lázaro Cárdenas no. 311, ☎2-01-05)* offers a big buffet near the bar and presents Mexican folk dancing, mariachi music and various other kinds of entertainment, including lassoers clad in *charros*, the traditional costume of Mexican rancheros.

 THE NORTHERN HOTEL ZONE

During the tourist season, a big *fiesta mexicana* is staged every Thursday night from 7pm to 10pm at the **Plaza Las Glorias**. It features cocktails, a Mexican buffet and folk-dance shows with mariachis.

**Christine's** *Avenida de las Garzas, Krystal Vallarta Hotel, ☎4-02-02)*, one of the most popular clubs in Puerto Vallarta, rocks the house with disco beats.

 MARINA VALLARTA

Everything, including romantic music, lends itself to relaxation at **El Faro** *(every day 5pm to 2am; Yates Club, ☎1-05-41)*, a club on the top floor of the seaside promenade's (Malecón)

ENTERTAINMENT

lighthouse, whence the view of the marina and Bahía de Banderas is magnificent.

**La Taberna** *(every day 10pm to 2am; Puesta del Sol, Room 1, ☎1-05-60)*, where the mood is set by the various televised sports games, boasts a comfortable terrace on the marina: The bar part surrounds one side of a large aquarium.

Bowling has its devotees in Vallarta. **Collage** *(10am to 2am; airport road, Marina Vallarta, ☎1-05-05)* is a vast complex that includes not only 18 bowling lanes and seven pool tables, but video games, a bar-restaurant and a dance hall with disco music.

The **Sazón** *(2nd floor, Las Iguanas shopping centre, ☎1-06-81 or 1-06-91)* is part discotheque and part restaurant. Its daring, dazzling modern decor makes it Puerto Vallarta's trendiest and most attractive night spot, which naturally means it's more expensive than other places. It's also a pretty good place to meet Mexicans.

 GAY BARS

**Los Balcones** *(Calle Juárez no. 186)*, a bar-nightclub, offers a view of teeming Juárez street. A large, brightly coloured dance floor takes up a good part of the premises. A few tables and couches near the bar attract a mixed clientele of both men and women. The establishment is very popular among Puerto Vallarta's gay community, which also hangs out at Paco Paco (see below) in the same neighbourhood.

From the street, you can see the umbrellas on the rooftop at **Paco Paco** *(Calle Ignacio L. Vallartas no. 278, ☎2-18-99)*. The nightclub on the ground floor plays American disco music amid dazzling strobe lights; upstairs, where there's a pool table, it's a little less noisy. The clientele is mixed.

Along the same lines, **Zotanos** *(7pm to 4am; facing the Río Cuale, in the park, just off the bridge)* has a bar on the ground floor and a nightclub in the basement.

# BULLS AND BULL FIGHTING

The **Plaza de Toros** *(100 pesos; Nov to May, Wed 5pm; Paseo de las Palmas, south of the Marina)* is Puerto Vallarta's bull fighting ring. Toreadors from all over the country stage bull-fights here, and four of the animals are killed during the course of the evening. You have to have a strong stomach and even be a bit bloodthirsty to enjoy this kind of spectacle, which nonetheless draws lots of tourists.

ENTERTAINMENT

## SHOPPING

**P**uerto Vallarta is packed with all manner of stores, catering to everyday needs as well as beautiful objects. Innumerable boutiques throughout the city reveal every aspect of Mexican culture. The main shopping areas are near the Malecón, on Morelos and Juárez streets and on the island in the Río Cuale. The least expensive places, however, lie south of the Río Cuale, on Insurgentes, Ignacio L. Vallarta and other streets in the area. Most of the big, modern hotels, as well as the Marina Vallarta, have shopping centres consisting of a variety of stores and stalls. Most places are open from 9am to 9pm.

 BOUTIQUES

### Isla Cuale and North of the Río Cuale

Don't miss the **Mercado Municipal** *(where the Río Cuale bridge meets Calle Agustín Rodríguez)*, an enormous flea market brimming with all types of merchandise: clothing, leather goods, handicrafts, magnificent chess boards, flamboyant papier-mâché parrots, hammocks and every cheap trinket imaginable.

---

### Handicrafts

Mexico's marvellous culture is reflected in its handicrafts. The indigenous peoples are especially talented in all forms of popular art and in all artistic disciplines: weaving, sculpture, pottery and painting. Many aboriginal artisans are grouped in cooperatives. Vendors, many of them natives, get their supplies from these cooperatives, or directly from artisans. They then resell the handcrafted goods in the big tourist centres or holiday resort areas.

Several boutiques in Puerto Vallarta are run by these cooperatives. Specializing in retail sales, they offer visitors the best prices, as well as a wide selection of magnificent works, including silver and gold pieces, dishes and colourful pottery, along with paintings, jewellery, fanciful wooden masks, fabrics, ceramics, blown glass, basketry, etc.

---

Next door, **México Artesanal** *(Calle Agustín Rodríguez no. 260, ☎3-09-25)* displays a wide selection of handicrafts, including pottery, dishes, glassware and handcrafted furniture painted in bright colours.

**Sol y Cactus** *(Calle Juárez no. 252, Puerto Vallarta, at the corner of Calle Guerrero, ☎2-13-46)* offers many blown-glass pieces. These pretty items come in a multitude of colours and shapes.

The **Galería de Artesanias Jalisciense** *(on Juárez street, facing Plaza de Armas)*, operated by the State of Jalisco, is the cheapest place to buy attractive items made by local artisans, including dishware, recycled glasses, pottery, all sorts of mobiles, etc.

The **Querubines** *(Calle Juárez no. 501)* is a pretty little store that sells a vast range of beautiful items. Colourful Guatemalan fabrics, tablecloths, napkins, braided carpets, masks fashioned from coconuts and painted gourds are piled up untidily and are sold at reasonable prices.

Aboriginal tapestries with beaded motifs are for sale at the magnificent **Galería de Arte Huichol** *(Calle Corona no. 164)*.

Some of the tapestries are made on the premises by talented native craftsmen.

Somewhat out of the way, north of Parque Hidalgo, **Alfarería Tlaquepaque** *(Avenida México no. 1100)* specializes in pottery and earthenware with an attractive brownish glaze. The boutique also offers glassware and trinkets. One entire wall is filled with reproductions of authentic Aztec and Mayan figurines.

## South of the Río Cuale

South of the Río Cuale, **La Rosa de Cristal** *(Calle Insurgentes no. 272,* ☎*2-56-98)* makes and sells, among other things, blown-glass items, earthenware, wrought-iron articles and reproductions of archaeological artifacts.

You can't visit Puerto Vallarta without stopping in at **Mundo de Azulejos** *(Calle Venustiano Carranza no. 374, at the corner of Calle Insurgentes,* ☎*2-26-75)*, the showroom for a manufacturer of a wide variety of gorgeous tiles and ceramics, as well as splendid wash basins. All the tiles are painted on the premises, and can be custom-decorated with inscriptions, drawings, a coat of arms and other designs.

## Northern Hotel Zone

Furniture-maker **Muebles Mexicanos** *(Foc. Medina Ascencio no. 1050, facing the Sheraton Buganvilias hotel,* ☎*2-28-00 or 2-17-15)* is worth the detour. It showcases the abilities and creative ingeniousness of regional cabinet-makers and crafts-men. Their work reflects major artistic talent. You can pur-chase, or merely admire, attractive chests of drawers and armoires with flower patterns carved into their panels, remark-able tables and chairs, as well as lovely hand-painted dishes.

SHOPPING

SHOPPING CENTRES

## Northern Hotel Zone

North of town, three shopping centres vie with one another for clients: **Plaza Villa Vallarta** and **Plaza Genovesa** *(both on Bulevar Francisco Medina Ascencio, Km 2)* and **Plaza Caracol** *(Bulevar Francisco Medina Ascencio, Km 2.5)*, the latter which attracts more locals than tourists because of its location near a residential area and its better prices.

## Marina Vallarta

**Plaza Marina** *(Carretera al Aeropuerto, Km 8)* is perhaps the largest shopping centre in the area, with specialized shops, businesses and offices of all kinds: home decoration, ready-to-wear clothing, shoes, stationer's, bookshop, art gallery, banks, exchange office, dry cleaner's, dental clinic, medical clinic, veterinary clinic, restaurants, souvenir stands, etc.

The smaller **Plaza Las Iguanas** shopping centre *(Manzana no. 10)* also houses a few lovely shops.

 ART GALLERIES

## The Old Town

**Isla Cuale and North of the Río Cuale**

In Puerto Vallarta, traditional Mexican art (paintings, clothing, jewellery, carpets, leather goods) from all over the country is sometimes exhibited alongside contemporary works. Some galleries stand out more than others. **Galería Uno** *(Morelos no. 561)* is one of these; on display here are works by contemporary Mexican and foreign artists who live in Puerto Vallarta at least six months a year.

**Museo Galería Manuel Lepe** *(Juárez no. 563)* highlights the life and work of the local-born painter. Manuel Lepe was Puerto Vallarta's master of naive painting, creating works imbued with colour, child-like exuberance and joy that are unquestionably very representative of his beloved city and its area, which he called *el paraíso*. The painter's murals also adorn certain municipal buildings in town.

On display at **Sergio Bustamante** *(Juárez no. 275, ☎3-14-05 or 2-54-80)* are the surrealist artist's jewellery, sculptures and models, made of everything from bronze and copper to ceramic and papier mâché. Often amusing, sometimes severe or rather strange, these creations leave no one indifferent. An absolute must-see!

**Galería de Arte Indígena** *(Juárez no. 270)* is located in what was Puerto Vallarta's first hotel. Certain sections upstairs are used for various exhibitions by Mexican and American artists. The gallery's pièce de résistance is the work of a young Huichol Indian artist: pottery decorated with tiny multicoloured glass beads. **Colección Huichol** *(every day 10am to 10pm; Morelos no. 490, ☎3-21-41)* and **Galería Muvieri** *(Mon to Sat 10am to 2pm and 5pm to 8pm; Libertad no. 177)* also specialize in Huichol art.

**Pueblo Real** *(Juárez no. 533)* was originally an arts centre run by Quebecer Claudio Tremblay. Though he is no longer with the centre, the works have been preserved in three galleries in the magnificent courtyard: **La Galería Principal**, where paintings by contemporary artists such as Rufino Tamayo and Sergio Cuevas are featured; **Galería Cava**, devoted to female artists, and **Guacha Bato**, which is also engraver Sergio Ruiz's studio. The rest of the building contains jewellery and handicraft shops as well as a café and a restaurant.

Other galleries also worth visiting include **Galería Anauak** *(Mon to Sat 10am to 2pm and 5pm to 9pm; Madero no. 268-B)*, which carries a collection of masks, pottery and pre-Colombian art; **Galería Rosas Blancas** *(Juárez no. 523)* and **Galería Vallarta** *(Mon to Sat 9:30am to 8pm; Juárez no. 263)*, which feature beautiful figurative and surrealist Mexican art pieces.

SHOPPING

**South of Río Cuale**

**Galería Pacifico** *(Mon to Sat 10am to 9pm, Sun 11am to 3pm; Insurgentes no. 109)* has been around for 10 years. The sculptures, paintings and posters on display here are the works of Mexican artists such as Ramiz Barquet, creator of *La Nostalgia*, which can be admired on the Malecón.

**Galería Dante** *(Mon to Sat 10am to 2pm and 6pm to 9pm; Basilio Badillo no. 269, ☎2-24-77)*, **Galería Olinalá** *(Mon to Sat 10am to 2pm and 5pm to 9pm; Lázaro Cárdenas no. 274)*, **Galería Piramide** *(Basilio Badillo no. 272)*, **Galería Pajaro** *(Aguiles Serdán no. 386)* and **Galería Parroquia** *(Mon to Sat 10am to 2pm and 4pm to 8pm; Independencia no. 231)* are several galleries where the magnificent works of prolific Mexican artists can be admired.

---

## Marina Vallarta

---

On the Marina Vallarta's *malecón*, **Arte de las Américas** *(every day 10am to 10pm; Las Palmas II)* carries an interesting hodgepodge of realist and surrealist works by both venerable and young up-and-coming artists. Two other galleries also worth checking out here are **Galería EM** *(Mon to Sat 10am to 2pm and 4pm to 10pm, Sun 6pm to 10pm; Las Palmas II no. 17)* and **Galería Javier Niño** *(Plaza Marina)*.

 ARTIST'S STUDIO

Jesús Botello Sánchez is unquestionably the most prolific and respected artist in Puerto Vallarta. His numerous works, which he signs "Tellosa", are awe-inspiring, whether they're paintings, murals, fountains or sculptures. They ornament the dining rooms and garden terraces of the best restaurants in the city, including the Café des Artistes, Cuiza and Santos. You can make an appointment to meet Jesús Botello Sánchez in his studio **Atelier Bezán** *(Guadalupe Sánchez no. 756, ☎2-30-12)*.

## ARTISTS' MATERIALS

Professional and amateur artists say that **Pro-Arte** *(México no.1197)* has the best selection of oils, canvases, easels, paints and gouaches. **Materiales para Artistas** *(Juárez no. 533)* has more of a selection, as well as beautiful lace table cloths.

 ## PHOTOGRAPHY

**Arco-Iris** *(Calle Juárez no. 602)* is undoubtedly the best bet for amateur or professional photographers.

 ## *PALETERÍAS* (ICE CREAM PARLOURS)

Puerto Vallarta's ice cream parlours all offer pretty much the same products. Coconut, pistachio, lemon, cheese and strawberry are among the most popular ice cream flavours, while *aguas de fruta*, frozen fruit juice on a stick, are among the most original creations. The main *paleterías* are downtown. **Paletería Muchuatana** *(at the corner of Morelos and Saragoza streets)* is the easiest to find, along with its neighbour across the main square *(Plaza de Armas)*. There's also an ice cream parlour on the Malecón *(Paseo Díaz Ordaz no. 556)*, and another a street away, the **Helados Paletas Bahía** *(Calle Juárez no. 528)*. The **Paletería la Flor de Michoacan** is located south of the Río Cuale *(at the corner of Insurgentes and Venustiano Carranza)*.

 ## *PANADERÍAS* (BAKERIES)

**Panadería Munguía** *(at the corner of Insurgentes and Aquiles Serdán, and on Juárez on the south side of the main square)* bakes a good loaf of bread, along with pastries, croissants and brioches. At the **Panadería Pili** *(Calle Lazaro Cárdenas no. 456)*, the fruit turnovers are absolutely delicious.

SHOPPING

WINES

Mexico produces red and white wines, mainly in Baja California. Since wine production is fairly limited, little wine is exported. Moreover, wine stores offering local vintages are rare. There is one place that sells excellent Mexican wines however: **Don Chui** *(Calle Aquiles Serdán no. 414, ☎3-02-86)*.

 FLORISTS

**Florería Paraíso** *(at the corner of Insurgentes and Lazaro Cárdenas; Calle Perú no. 1226)* and **Florería Vallarta** *(Mon to Sat, 9am to 9pm, Plaza Genovesa, hotel zone)* offer a wide choice of cut flowers and potted plants to perk up your room or studio apartment, for a birthday or anniversary, to offer Mexican friends or simply to take home a magnificent bouquet of tropical flowers. Be aware that on your return to North America, only cut flowers are allowed through customs; potted plants containing earth will likely be confiscated on the spot!

 GROCERY STORES AND FOOD MARKETS

These big stores also sell hardware items, stationary, pharmaceutical items and clothing. In other words, you can find everything in them, from clothes to Mexican and American magazines. **Gutiérrez Rizo** *(corner of Aquiles Serdán and Constitución)* and **Plaza Ley** *(corner of Avenida México and Calle Uruguay)*, downtown, just south of the Río Cuale, offer lots of Mexican and North American produce (fresh or canned). Its baked goods have a fine reputation and its counters covered with peppers are very impressive. An entire section is devoted to local wines and vintages imported from Chile and Spain. The **Gigante** *(Plaza Caracol, north of the Sheraton hotel)* is similar, but also has a fish shop. The Marina Vallarta's grocery store is the **Comercial Mexicana** *(Plaza Genovesa and Plaza Marina)*.

---

# GLOSSARY

---

**Several tips on Spanish pronunciation in Latin America.**

## CONSONANTS

*b*     Is pronounced **b** or sometimes a soft **v**, depending on the region or the person: *bizcocho* (biz-koh-choh or viz-koh-choh).

*c*     As in English, *c* is pronounced as **s** before *i* and *e*: *cerro* (seh-rroh). When it is placed in front of other vowels, it is hard and pronounced as **k**: *carro* (kah-rroh). The *c* is also hard when it comes before a consonant, except before an *h* (see further below).

*d*     Is pronounced like a soft **d**: *dar* (dahr). *D* is usually not pronounced when at the end of a word.

*g*     As with the *c*, *g* is soft before an *i* or an *e*, and is pronounced like a soft **h**: *gente* (hente). In front of other vowels and consonants, the *g* is hard: *golf* (pronounced the same way as in English).

*ch*     Pronounced **ch**, as in English: *leche* (le-che). Like the *ll*, this combination is considered a single letter in the Spanish alphabet, listed separately in dictionaries and telephone directories.

*h*     Is not pronounced: *hora* (oh-ra).

*j*     Is pronounced like a guttural **h**, as in "him".

*ll*     Is pronounced like a hard **y**, as in "yes": *llamar* (yah-mar). In some regions, such as central Colombia, *ll* is pronounced as a soft **g**, as in "mirage" (*Medellín* is pronounced Medegin). Like the *ch*, this combination is considered a single letter in the Spanish alphabet, and is listed separately in dictionaries and telephone directories.

ñ    Is pronounced like the **ni** in "onion", or the **ny** in "canyon": *señora* (seh-nyo-rah).

qu   Is pronounced **k**: *aquí* (ah-kee).

r    Is rolled, as the Irish or Italian pronunciation of **r**.

s    Is always pronounced **s** like "sign": *casa* (cah-ssah).

v    Is pronounced like a **b**: *vino* (bee-noh).

z    Is pronounced like **s**: *paz* (pahss).

### VOWELS

a    Is always pronounced **ah** as in "part", and never *ay* as in "day": *faro* (fah-roh).

e    Is pronounced **eh** as in "elf," and never *ey* as in "grey or "ee" as in "key": *helado* (eh-lah-doh].

i    Is always pronounced **ee**: *cine* (see-neh).

o    Is always pronounced **oh** as in "cone": *copa* (koh-pah).

u    Is always pronounced **oo**: *universidad* (oo-nee-ver-see-dah).

**All other letters are pronounced the same as in English.**

### STRESSING SYLLABLES

In Spanish, syllables are differently stressed. This stress is very important, and emphasizing the right syllable might even be necessary to make yourself understood. If a vowel has an accent, this syllable is the one that should be stressed. If there is no accent, follow this rule:

Stress the second-last syllable of any word that ends with a vowel: *amigo.*

Stress the last syllable of any word that ends in a consonant, except for **s** (plural of nouns and adjectives) or **n** (plural of nouns): *usted* (but *amigos*, *hablan*).

**GREETINGS**

| | |
|---|---|
| Goodbye | *adiós, hasta luego* |
| Good afternoon and good evening | *buenas tardes* |
| Hi (casual) | *hola* |
| Good morning | *buenos días* |
| Good night | *buenas noches* |
| Thank-you | *gracias* |
| Please | *por favor* |
| You are welcome | *de nada* |
| Excuse me | *perdone/a* |
| My name is... | *mi nombre es...* |
| What is your name? | *¿cómo se llama usted?* |
| yes | *no* |
| no | *sí* |
| Do you speak English? | *¿habla usted inglés?* |
| Slower, please | *más despacio, por favor* |
| I am sorry, I don't speak Spanish | *Lo siento, no hablo español* |
| | |
| How are you? | *¿qué tal?* |
| I am fine | *estoy bien* |
| | |
| I am American (male/female) | *Soy estadounidense* |
| I am Australian | *Soy autraliano/a* |
| I am Belgian | *Soy belga* |
| I am British (male/female) | *Soy británico/a* |
| I am Canadian | *Soy canadiense* |
| I am German (male/female) | *Soy alemán/a* |
| I am Italian (male/female) | *Soy italiano/a* |
| I am Swiss | *Soy suizo* |
| I am a tourist | *Soy turista* |
| | |
| single (m/f) | *soltero/a* |
| divorced (m/f) | *divorciado/a* |
| married (m/f) | *casado/a* |
| friend (m/f) | *amigo/a* |
| child (m/f) | *niño/a* |
| husband, wife | *esposo/a* |
| mother | *madre* |
| father | *padre* |
| brother, sister | *hermano/a* |
| widower widow | *viudo/a* |
| | |
| I am hungry | *tengo hambre* |
| I am ill | *estoy enfermo/a* |

| | |
|---|---|
| I am thirsty | *tengo sed* |

## DIRECTIONS

| | |
|---|---|
| beside | *al lado de* |
| to the right | *a la derecha* |
| to the left | *a la izquierda* |
| here | *aquí* |
| there | *allí* |
| into, inside | *dentro* |
| outside | *fuera* |
| behind | *detrás* |
| in front of | *delante* |
| between | *entre* |
| far from | *lejos de* |
| Where is ... ? | *¿dónde está ... ?* |
| To get to ...? | *¿para ir a...?* |
| near | *cerca de* |
| straight ahead | *todo recto* |

## MONEY

| | |
|---|---|
| money | *dinero / plata* |
| credit card | *tarjeta de crédito* |
| exchange | *cambio* |
| traveller's cheque | *cheque de viaje* |
| I don't have any money | *no tengo dinero* |
| The bill, please | *la cuenta, por favor* |
| receipt | *recibo* |

## SHOPPING

| | |
|---|---|
| store | *tienda* |
| market | *mercado* |
| open | *abierto/a* |
| closed | *cerrado/a* |
| How much is this? | *¿cuánto es?* |
| to buy | *comprar* |
| to sell | *vender* |
| the customer | *el / la cliente* |
| salesman | *vendedor* |
| saleswoman | *vendedora* |
| I need... | *necesito...* |
| I would like... | *yo quisiera...* |
| | |
| batteries | *pilas* |
| blouse | *blusa* |

| | |
|---|---|
| cameras | *cámaras* |
| cosmetics and perfumes | *cosméticos y perfumes* |
| cotton | *algodón* |
| dress jacket | *saco* |
| eyeglasses | *lentes, gafas* |
| fabric | *tela* |
| film | *película* |
| gifts | *regalos* |
| gold | *oro* |
| handbag | *bolsa* |
| hat | *sombrero* |
| jewellery | *joyería* |
| leather | *cuero, piel* |
| local crafts | *artesanía* |
| magazines | *revistas* |
| newpapers | *periódicos* |
| pants | *pantalones* |
| records, cassettes | *discos, casetas* |
| sandals | *sandalias* |
| shirt | *camisa* |
| shoes | *zapatos* |
| silver | *plata* |
| skirt | *falda* |
| sun screen products | *productos solares* |
| T-shirt | *camiseta* |
| watch | *reloj* |
| wool | *lana* |

## MISCELLANEOUS

| | |
|---|---|
| a little | *poco* |
| a lot | *mucho* |
| good (m/f) | *bueno/a* |
| bad (m/f) | *malo/a* |
| beautiful (m/f) | *hermoso/a* |
| pretty (m/f) | *bonito/a* |
| ugly | *feo* |
| big | *grande* |
| tall (m/f) | *alto/a* |
| small (m/f) | *pequeño/a* |
| short (length) (m/f) | *corto/a* |
| short (person) (m/f) | *bajo/a* |
| cold (m/f) | *frío/a* |
| hot | *caliente* |
| dark (m/f) | *oscuro/a* |

GLOSSARY

| light (colour) | *claro* |
| do not touch | *no tocar* |
| expensive (m/f) | *caro/a* |
| cheap (m/f) | *barato/a* |
| fat (m/f) | *gordo/a* |
| slim, skinny (m/f) | *delgado/a* |
| heavy (m/f) | *pesado/a* |
| light (weight) (m/f) | *ligero/a* |
| less | *menos* |
| more | *más* |
| narrow (m/f) | *estrecho/a* |
| wide (m/f) | *ancho/a* |
| new (m/f) | *nuevo/a* |
| old (m/f) | *viejo/a* |
| nothing | *nada* |
| something (m/f) | *algo/a* |
| quickly | *rápidamente* |
| slowly (m/f) | *despacio/a* |
| What is this? | *¿qué es esto?* |
| when? | *¿cuando?* |
| where? | *¿dónde?* |

## TIME

| in the afternoon, early evening | *por la tarde* |
| at night | *por la noche* |
| in the daytime | *por el día* |
| in the morning | *por la mañana* |
| minute | *minuto* |
| month | *mes* |
| ever | *jamás* |
| never | *nunca* |
| now | *ahora* |
| today | *hoy* |
| yesterday | *ayer* |
| tomorrow | *mañana* |
| What time is it? | *¿qué hora es?* |
| hour | *hora* |
| week | *semana* |
| year | *año* |

| Sunday | *domingo* |
| Monday | *lunes* |
| Tuesday | *martes* |
| Wednesday | *miércoles* |

| | |
|---|---|
| Thursday | *jueves* |
| Friday | *viernes* |
| Saturday | *sábado* |
| January | *enero* |
| February | *febrero* |
| March | *marzo* |
| April | *abril* |
| May | *mayo* |
| June | *junio* |
| July | *julio* |
| August | *agosto* |
| September | *septiembre* |
| October | *octubre* |
| November | *noviembre* |
| December | *diciembre* |

## WEATHER

| | |
|---|---|
| It is cold | *hace frío* |
| It is warm | *hace calor* |
| It is very hot | hace mucho calor |
| sun | *sol* |
| It is sunny | hace sol |
| It is cloudy | *está nublado* |
| rain | *lluvia* |
| It is raining | *está lloviendo* |
| wind | *viento* |
| It is windy | *hay viento* |
| snow | *nieve* |
| damp | *húmedo* |
| dry | *seco* |
| storm | *tormenta* |
| hurricane | *huracán* |

## COMMUNICATION

| | |
|---|---|
| air mail | *correos aéreo* |
| collect call | *llamada por cobrar* |
| dial the number | *marcar el número* |
| area code, country code | *código* |
| envelope | *sobre* |
| long distance | *larga distancia* |
| post office | *correo* |
| rate | *tarifa* |
| stamps | *estampillas* |
| telegram | *telegrama* |

| | |
|---|---|
| telephone book | *un guia telefónica* |
| wait for the tone | *esperar la señal* |

## ACTIVITIES

| | |
|---|---|
| beach | *playa* |
| museum or gallery | *museo* |
| scuba diving | *buceo* |
| to swim | *bañarse* |
| to walk around | *pasear* |
| hiking | *caminata* |
| trail | *pista, sendero* |
| cycling | *ciclismo* |
| fishing | *pesca* |

## TRANSPORTATION

| | |
|---|---|
| arrival | *llegada* |
| departure | *salida* |
| on time | *a tiempo* |
| cancelled (m/f) | *anulado/a* |
| one way ticket | *ida* |
| return | *regreso* |
| round trip | *ida y vuelta* |
| schedule | *horario* |
| baggage | *equipajes* |
| north | *norte* |
| south | *sur* |
| east | *este* |
| west | *oeste* |
| avenue | *avenida* |
| street | *calle* |
| highway | *carretera* |
| expressway | *autopista* |
| airplane | *avión* |
| airport | *aeropuerto* |
| bicycle | *bicicleta* |
| boat | *barco* |
| bus | *bus* |
| bus stop | *parada* |
| bus terminal | *terminal* |
| train | *tren* |
| train crossing | *crucero ferrocarril* |
| station | *estación* |
| neighbourhood | *barrio* |
| collective taxi | *colectivo* |

| | |
|---|---|
| corner | *esquina* |
| express | *rápido* |
| safe | *seguro/a* |
| be careful | *cuidado* |
| car | *coche, carro* |
| To rent a car | *alquilar un auto* |
| gas | *gasolina* |
| gas station | *gasolinera* |
| no parking | *no estacionar* |
| no passing | *no adelantar* |
| parking | *parqueo* |
| pedestrian | *peaton* |
| road closed, no through traffic | *no hay paso* |
| slow down | *reduzca velocidad* |
| speed limit | *velocidad permitida* |
| stop | *alto* |
| stop! (an order) | *pare* |
| traffic light | *semáforo* |

## ACCOMMODATION

| | |
|---|---|
| cabin, bungalow | *cabaña* |
| accommodation | *alojamiento* |
| double, for two people | *doble* |
| single, for one person | *sencillo* |
| high season | *temporada alta* |
| low season | *temporada baja* |
| bed | *cama* |
| floor (first, second...) | *piso* |
| main floor | *planta baja* |
| manager | *gerente, jefe* |
| double bed | *cama matrimonial* |
| cot | *camita* |
| bathroom | *baños* |
| with private bathroom | *con baño privado* |
| hot water | *agua caliente* |
| breakfast | *desayuno* |
| elevator | *ascensor* |
| air conditioning | *aire acondicionado* |
| fan | *ventilador, abanico* |
| pool | *piscina, alberca* |
| room | *habitación* |

**NUMBERS**

| | | | |
|---|---|---|---|
| 1 | *uno* | 30 | *treinta* |
| 2 | *dos* | 31 | *treinta y uno* |
| 3 | *tres* | 32 | *treinta y dos* |
| 4 | *cuatro* | 40 | *cuarenta* |
| 5 | *cinco* | 50 | *cincuenta* |
| 6 | *seis* | 60 | *sesenta* |
| 7 | *siete* | 70 | *setenta* |
| 8 | *ocho* | 80 | *ochenta* |
| 9 | *nueve* | 90 | *noventa* |
| 10 | *diez* | 100 | *cien* |
| 11 | *once* | 101 | *ciento uno* |
| 12 | *doce* | 102 | *ciento dos* |
| 13 | *trece* | 200 | *doscientos* |
| 14 | *catorce* | 300 | *trescientos* |
| 15 | *quince* | 400 | *quatrocientoa* |
| 16 | *dieciséis* | 500 | *quinientos* |
| 17 | *diecisiete* | 600 | *seiscientos* |
| 18 | *dieciocho* | 700 | *sietecientos* |
| 19 | *diecinueve* | 800 | *ochocientos* |
| 20 | *veinte* | 900 | *novecientos* |
| 21 | *veintiuno* | 1,000 | *mil* |
| 22 | *veintidós* | 1,100 | *mil cien* |
| 23 | *veintitrés* | 1,200 | *mil doscientos* |
| 24 | *veinticuatro* | 2000 | *dos mil* |
| 25 | *veinticinco* | 3000 | *tres mil* |
| 26 | *veintiséis* | 10,000 | *diez mil* |
| 27 | *veintisiete* | 100,000 | *cien mil* |
| 28 | *veintiocho* | 1,000,000 | *un millón* |
| 29 | *veintinueve* | | |

# INDEX

INDEX

TRAVEL
BETTER...
TRAVEL
THE NET

Visit our web site
to travel better...
to discover, to explore
and to enjoy more

# www.ulysses.ca

Catalogue

Talk to us

Order

Distributors

History

Internet
Travel

# Travel Notes

## ORDER FORM

### ULYSSES TRAVEL GUIDES

| | | | | |
|---|---|---|---|---|
| ☐ Atlantic Canada | $24.95 CAN<br>$17.95 US | ☐ Lisbon | $18.95 CAN<br>$13.95 US | |
| ☐ Bahamas | $24.95 CAN<br>$17.95 US | ☐ Louisiana | $29.95 CAN<br>$21.95 US | |
| ☐ Beaches of Maine | $12.95 CAN<br>$9.95 US | ☐ Martinique | $24.95 CAN<br>$17.95 US | |
| ☐ Bed & Breakfasts<br>in Québec | $13.95 CAN<br>$10.95 US | ☐ Montréal | $19.95 CAN<br>$14.95 US | |
| ☐ Belize | $16.95 CAN<br>$12.95 US | ☐ New Orleans | $17.95 CAN<br>$12.95 US | |
| ☐ Calgary | $17.95 CAN<br>$12.95 US | ☐ New York City | $19.95 CAN<br>$14.95 US | |
| ☐ Canada | $29.95 CAN<br>$21.95 US | ☐ Nicaragua | $24.95 CAN<br>$16.95 US | |
| ☐ Chicago | $19.95 CAN<br>$14.95 US | ☐ Ontario | $27.95 CAN<br>$19.95US | |
| ☐ Chile | $27.95 CAN<br>$17.95 US | ☐ Ottawa | $17.95 CAN<br>$12.95 US | |
| ☐ Colombia | $29.95 CAN<br>$21.95 US | ☐ Panamá | $24.95 CAN<br>$17.95 US | |
| ☐ Costa Rica | $27.95 CAN<br>$19.95 US | ☐ Peru | $27.95 CAN<br>$19.95 US | |
| ☐ Cuba | $24.95 CAN<br>$17.95 US | ☐ Portugal | $24.95 CAN<br>$16.95 US | |
| ☐ Dominican<br>Republic | $24.95 CAN<br>$17.95 US | ☐ Provence -<br>Côte d'Azur | $29.95 CAN<br>$21.95US | |
| ☐ Ecuador and<br>Galapagos Islands | $24.95 CAN<br>$17.95 US | ☐ Québec | $29.95 CAN<br>$21.95 US | |
| ☐ El Salvador | $22.95 CAN<br>$14.95 US | ☐ Québec and<br>Ontario with Via | $9.95 CAN<br>$7.95 US | |
| ☐ Guadeloupe | $24.95 CAN<br>$17.95 US | ☐ Toronto | $18.95 CAN<br>$13.95 US | |
| ☐ Guatemala | $24.95 CAN<br>$17.95 US | ☐ Vancouver | $17.95 CAN<br>$12.95 US | |
| ☐ Honduras | $24.95 CAN<br>$17.95 US | ☐ Washington D.C. | $18.95 CAN<br>$13.95 US | |
| ☐ Jamaica | $24.95 CAN<br>$17.95 US | ☐ Western Canada | $29.95 CAN<br>$21.95 US | |

### ULYSSES DUE SOUTH

| | | | |
|---|---|---|---|
| ☐ Acapulco | $14.95 CAN<br>$9.95 US | ☐ Cartagena<br>(Colombia) | $12.95 CAN<br>$9.95 US |
| ☐ Belize | $16.95 CAN<br>$12.95 US | ☐ Cancun Cozumel | $17.95 CAN<br>$12.95 US |

## ULYSSES DUE SOUTH

☐ Puerto Vallarta . $14.95 CAN
$9.95 US

☐ St. Martin and . $16.95 CAN
St. Barts $12.95 US

## ULYSSES TRAVEL JOURNAL

☐ Ulysses Travel . $9.95 CAN
Journal $7.95 US
(Blue, Red, Green,
Yellow, Sextant)

☐ Ulysses Travel $14.95 CAN
Journal 80 Days $9.95 US

## ULYSSES GREEN ESCAPES

☐ Cycling in France $22.95 CAN
$16.95 US
☐ Cycling in Ontario $22.95 CAN
$16.95 US

☐ Hiking in the . . . $19.95 CAN
Northeastern U.S. $13.95 US
☐ Hiking in Québec $19.95 CAN
$13.95 US

| TITLE | QUANTITY | PRICE | TOTAL |
|---|---|---|---|
|  |  |  |  |
|  |  |  |  |
|  |  |  |  |
|  |  |  |  |
|  |  |  |  |

| | |
|---|---|
| Name _____ | Sub-total |
| Address _____ | Postage & Handling — $8.00* |
| _____ | |
| _____ | Sub-total |
| Payment : ☐ Money Order ☐ Visa ☐ MasterCard | G.S.T. in Canada 7% |
| Card Number _____ | |
| Signature _____ | TOTAL |

**ULYSSES TRAVEL PUBLICATIONS**
4176 St-Denis,
Montréal, Québec, H2W 2M5
(514) 843-9447 fax (514) 843-9448
www.ulysses.ca
* $15 for overseas orders

U.S. ORDERS: **GLOBE PEQUOT PRESS**
P.O. Box 833, 6 Business Park Road,
Old Saybrook, CT 06475-0833
1-800-243-0495 fax 1-800-820-2329
www.globe-pequot.com